CATHERINE of SIENA

A BIOGRAPHY

Anne B. Baldwin

D1056221

hing Division
r, Inc.
46750

ACKNOWLEDGMENTS: Scripture texts contained in this work are quoted from the *New American Bible*, © 1970 by the Confraternity of Christian Doctrine, Washington, D.C., all rights reserved. Other sources from which material has been excerpted or has served as the basis for portions of this work are cited in the Bibliography, among them: *The Dialogue*, by Catherine Benincasa, translated by Suzanne Noffke, O.P. (Paulist Press, © 1980); *The Life of Catherine of Siena*, by Raymond of Capua [under his family name, deVigne], translated by Conleth Kearns, O.P. (Michael Glazier, Inc., © 1980); also the same work as translated by George Lamb (reprinted with permission of Macmillan Publishing Company, translation © 1960 by Harvill Press and Macmillan Publishing Company); *Saint Catherine of Siena*, by Johannes Jorgensen, translated by Ingeborg Lund (Longmans, Green & Co., © 1938); and *Saint Catherine of Siena as Seen in Her Letters*, by Vida Scudder (E.P. Dutton & Co., © 1926). The author is grateful to the copyright holders for the use of their materials. If any copyrighted materials have been inadvertently used in this book without proper credit being given, please notify Our Sunday Visitor in writing so that future printings of this work may be corrected accordingly.

PHOTO SECTION: The photographs appearing in this work are reproduced from *Saint Catherine of Siena and Her Times*, by M.D. Roberts (G.P. Putnam's Sons, © 1906), courtesy of Phillips Memorial Library, Providence College, Providence, R.I.

Copyright © 1987 by Our Sunday Visitor Publishing Division
Our Sunday Visitor, Inc.
ALL RIGHTS RESERVED

With the exception of short excerpts for critical reviews, no part of this book may be reproduced in any manner whatsoever without permission in writing from the publisher. Write:
Our Sunday Visitor Publishing Division
Our Sunday Visitor, Inc.
200 Noll Plaza
Huntington, Indiana 46750

International Standard Book Number: 0-87973-510-4
Library of Congress Catalog Card Number: 86-63595

Cover design by James E. McIlrath based on original print of Saint Catherine of Siena by Francesco Vanni

PRINTED IN THE UNITED STATES OF AMERICA

TO BOB

Contents

PART ONE

□

Catherine
Then

1

The Childhood of a Saint

Two young children were walking home through the streets of Siena one evening in 1352. They had been visiting their married sister Buonaventura, who lived on the outskirts of town, near the San Ansano Gate.

The boy, Stephen Benincasa, rushed ahead with the explosive energy of a healthy eight-year-old. The girl, Catherine, walked slowly, savoring the memory of her afternoon with Buonaventura. She loved being at her sister's house. It was quiet there, and peaceful. There were meadows all around, full of butterflies and birds, beautiful things to see and hear. A girl could think her own thoughts there or stare at a flower without interruption.

It was not like that at home, in the heart of the city, where her large family shared a house with her father's dye business.

Giacomo and Lapa Benincasa, the girl's parents, were a prosperous couple. They had been successful. Twelve of their twenty-five children had survived infancy, and most of those twelve still lived at home, along with the wives of the older sons, as well as the family servant and the dye workers.

Giacomo had built a fine sturdy house to accommodate them all on Via dei Tintori (Street of the Dyers), near the well known as Fontebranda. It was a house a man could be proud to own, but it was not a peaceful place to live.

Acrid fumes rose from the dye works on the first floor, filling the house and spilling out into the street. Equally sharp and penetrating was the voice of Giacomo's wife, Lapa, who ran the lives of all the household, shouting out orders from dawn to dusk and on into the night.

Little Catherine did not rush back to the bustle of that house on Via dei Tintori. With her heart at peace after her visit to the country, she walked slowly, watching the changing colors of the evening sky. The road led down a steep flight of steps with a clear view of the valley beyond. Catherine paused there at the turning of the steps, looked out across the valley toward the great cathedral of San Domenico, and saw a vision that would change her life.

She saw Jesus Christ Himself, dressed as a pope, with beautiful gold-embroidered vestments and the great papal tiara. He was seated on a throne, and the Apostles Peter and Paul and John the Evangelist stood beside Him. But Jesus was not looking at them; He was looking directly at Catherine, smiling at her, loving her. While she stood and stared, wondering at His love, Jesus stepped toward her and blessed her, making the Sign of the Cross over her. She gazed at Him with the eyes of body and soul and was transported out of herself. She lost all consciousness of herself and her surroundings, aware only of Him and His love that filled her soul with a comfort she had never known. As she basked in the warmth of that love, she yearned to please Him who loved her so. Whatever He asked of her, she would do.

In the meantime, Stephen went on ahead, assuming that his younger sister was not far behind. When he realized that he was alone, he turned back to find her and saw her standing in the roadway, gazing up toward heaven. He yelled to her to hurry along, but she made no move. Exasperated he ran back to where she stood, shouting to her all the time, and when she still made no response, he shook her, hard. "What are you doing here? Come on, we have got to get home!" he cried.

Catherine spoke like someone roused out of a deep sleep. "If you could see what I see," she said, "you would never try to disturb me." She glanced at Stephen for just a moment and then raised her eyes again to recapture the vision, but it had vanished. She burst into tears, angry with herself for allowing her eyes to look away from the wonderful sight, even for a moment.

Catherine was just six years old when she saw this vision, but her childhood had ended. Our Lord had issued an invitation to her to love Him and to be loved by Him, and she responded to that invitation with a "yes" that came from the very depth of her young being, a "yes" that had to be affirmed and reaffirmed throughout her life, a "yes" that would allow Jesus to train and strengthen her until she became one of the greatest saints the Church has ever seen. But when she went home, she did not tell anyone what had happened.

From all reports she was a happy child, a beautiful child, with shiny golden curls that everyone admired. Some people used the word "euphoric" to describe her bubbly nature as a very young child. When neighbors visited the sick, they would ask to take Catherine along because she was so good at cheering people.

She liked to be alone, something that was not easy on Via dei Tintori. When she played with other children, she usually dominated them, persuading them to play her way.

Catherine's way, usually, was to play "saint," or even better, "holy hermit." When she was by herself, she would find a dark corner of that big house, the back of a stairwell, perhaps, and pretend it was a cave where she could withdraw and pray and fast for hours. In her hidden place she would scourge her young body with a special knotted rope; this scourging was a form of penance commonly called "the discipline" and widely practiced by holy people of her day.

When she was with other children, she taught them to pray, too. She taught them the Our Father and the Hail Mary, how to kneel and how to fast. She even introduced them to her special rope that they used on one another.

In time Catherine became impatient with this sort of fantasy play and began to yearn for the real thing. She set out one morning to find a cave where she could start her life as a hermit. With a loaf of bread under her arm, she took a road out beyond Buonaventura's house, beyond the great city wall and the San Ansano Gate, out to a deserted area where rocky embankments were studded with caves. When she found one that seemed right for her purpose, she knelt down and began to pray. Soon she was swept up into a state of ecstatic prayer in which she lost awareness of her surroundings and even of her own body.

Some time later Catherine woke with a start, confused at first as to where she was and why she was there. She was dizzy and her knees felt weak. She wished she were home. She wondered how long she had been away and whether her parents were worried about her. She set out for home right away, hurrying as fast as she could in her weakened condition, vowing that never again would she put her parents through such an ordeal. The sun was already setting. Maybe the city gate would close before she got there. Maybe she would have to spend all night out in this wilderness, with her parents worried and upset. The next thing she knew she was safely inside the city gate and soon was back among her family who, in fact, had not even been worried about her. They thought she had gone to visit Buonaventura, and assumed — coincidentally, in this case — that she would be back before it got dark.

She was back, but she was changed. During the prayer in the cave, something immense had happened to Catherine. Her friends and biographers — Raymond of Capua (who eventually would be beatified), Father Tommaso Caffarini, and others — gave conflicting reports on what they understood to have happened. But all agreed on two points: she never again tried to live as a hermit, and after this cave experience she became very concerned with virginity.

She was entering a new phase of her relationship with her Lord. The "yes" she spoke when she saw that first vision of Jesus, was spoken again, but with a little more maturity and a little more understanding of what Christ was asking of her. She felt a great desire to be more fully united with Jesus, to belong to Him, to serve Him, to be His bride. She saw clearly how the cares of this earth and her earthly body could distract her and take her mind off her loving Savior. She thought about the words of Saint Paul, "The virgin — indeed, any unmarried woman — is concerned with things of the Lord, in pursuit of holiness in body and spirit. The married woman, on the other hand, has the cares of this world to absorb her and is concerned with pleasing her husband" (1 Corinthians 7:34).

Catherine wanted to pursue "holiness in body and spirit"; this seven-year-old was determined to remain a virgin for her Lord Jesus Christ. She turned to the Queen of Virgins for guidance and intercession.

One day she prayed, "Most blessed and most sacred Virgin, . . . overlook my unworthiness and my nothingness, and graciously grant me this great favor — to give me as my Spouse the One I long for from my inmost heart, your own all-holy and only Son, our Lord Jesus Christ; and I promise Him and promise you that . . . I too will keep my virginity forever spotless for Him."[1]

She saw a vision of Mary together with her Son, bathed in heavenly light. As her prayer continued, she saw Mary present Jesus to her. From that day Catherine considered herself engaged to Jesus.

She wanted to be a suitable bride. She felt she had to deny the promptings of her own selfish, self-indulgent will, so she could submit herself better to the will of her Beloved. She began to discipline her body, denying its desires and cravings. As

11

Raymond of Capua put it, "The little disciple of Christ began to fight against the flesh before the flesh had begun to rebel."[2]

She gave up eating meat, as far as she could, and when she was served meat, she passed it on to her brother Stephen or threw it to the cats under the table. She increased the severity of "the discipline" she practiced upon herself, either alone or with the other children. With all of this she developed a concern for souls and a love for saints who gave their lives for the salvation of others.

All of this was a secret life. The adults around her did not notice anything unusual about Catherine's behavior. She seemed to play as any little girl might play. A child could assume any sort of fantasy role: she could play "mother," or "king and queen," or "saint." Catherine chose most often to play "saint." There was nothing remarkable about that, not for a child growing up in her culture. Catherine was doing what all children do when they play — she was incorporating into her games the life she saw around her and the stories she heard told.

Her relatives were pious people to whom God and the Church were very important. Catherine's father was a quiet and saintly man known for his patience, his integrity, and his dislike of profanity. Lapa liked to tell how he dealt with a man who nearly brought the family to ruin by falsely claiming that Giacomo owed him money. Many men living in Siena in the 1300s would have responded to such lies with murder, starting a blood feud. But not Giacomo Benincasa. He told his family to trust in God and to pray for the liar. "God will show him the error of his ways and be our defender," he told his family, and he was right. In time the truth came out, and Giacomo's reputation was restored, as were his fortunes.

No one considered Lapa saintly, though there is heroism and tragedy in a woman who bears twenty-five children and buries most of them. Those who knew her described her as loud and not very smart. Raymond of Capua, who never criticized anyone who loved Catherine, said that although Lapa "may have lacked the shrewdness of the people of today, she was quite capable of looking after a home and family."[3]

"Simple Lapa" they called her, especially when she was bewildered by her brilliant and saintly daughter whom she loved, but never understood.

In fourteenth-century Siena the family was very important. Uncles and aunts, cousins and in-laws — all were a source of strength in time of civil disturbance, and often a source of money for a man starting a new business. These ties provided the strong social fabric that held the family together and shaped the lives of all.

The Benincasa family included priests and nuns, members of the Third Order of Saint Dominic (known popularly as the Mantellate), and even one canonized saint, John Colombini, whose niece, Lisa, married Catherine's brother Bartolommeo.

All of these were people of great faith. Family life was filled with prayer, attendance at Mass, a belief in miracles, and retelling the stories of saints, especially saints from that region.

Catherine never went to school, was never taught to read. Daughters of merchants, even prosperous merchants, were not educated in the fourteenth century. Yet Catherine hungered for knowledge, especially knowledge of God and the saints. Like young people of all ages, she was learning how she should live. She did not see her mother as a model to follow. She looked to the saints instead. They were the heroes of her age. They were the people to imitate.

She sought out knowledge of the saints everywhere she could find it. When she went to church, she studied the stained-glass windows and the statues. She listened intently to the readings at Mass as well as to the prayers and sermons. At home she heard the stories of the local saints.

Most satisfying of all to her young mind were the tales

she heard from *The Golden Legend*, a collection of stories about the saints of the Church calendar, compiled by Jacobus de Voragine for use by priests preparing their sermons. Jacobus collected and published all the stories he could find, never weeding out those that were clearly untrue or illogical. In his work Christians stand side by side with satyrs and centaurs, the possible and the impossible given equal dignity. The inspired wisdom of the desert Fathers is included along with sentimental fantasies about the childhood of Jesus. But the theme that recurs most often in *The Golden Legend* is that the saints proved their love for Jesus by accepting humiliation, torture, and death.

Too young to distinguish truth from fantasy, Catherine listened hungrily to it all. Many of the stories were vivid and bloodcurdling. There was the tale, for instance, of two young Christians of the third century who were seized by the Emperor Decius, a man notorious for his bloodthirsty persecution of Christians. One of the young men was stripped, coated with honey, and left to hang in the blazing sun, tormented by bees and hornets. But he never denied Jesus.

His companion was bound hand and foot to a luxurious bed, in a sumptuous setting, where perfume and sensual music filled the air. A lewd and voluptuous woman was sent in to arouse him sexually and take his mind off his pure love for Jesus. The youth, though his hands and feet were bound, found one last defense. Biting off his tongue in desperation, he spat it out at the woman and then rejoiced as the pain saved him from seduction.

Stories like these had a powerful influence on popular belief of the time and on Catherine. These tales came into her life through young Tommaso della Fonte, a nephew whom Giacomo adopted after the boy's parents died in the Black Death, the plague that killed millions throughout Europe. Tommaso was studying for the priesthood when he came to the Benincasa home. He enjoyed reading *The Golden Legend* to his uncle's family and especially to young Catherine. The stories filled her evenings and fed her imagination. They gave her a heroic model to think about and act out in her fantasies. They helped her through her childhood.

A quiet child, born of a very vocal mother who did not understand her need for silence, a child with a need for solitude living in a crowded house, Catherine became adept at withdrawing into prayer. In prayer she could again be with her Beloved and His holy Mother; in prayer she experienced bliss. No one in her family quite realized what was happening, not even Catherine; but her play and prayer were becoming inseparable, and together they were transforming a little girl into a strong servant of God.

The "yes" her heart spoke to Jesus at the age of six had never been retracted. On the contrary, it had been repeated and strengthened. The decision she made to remain a virgin for Jesus' sake likewise remained a solemn commitment. Catherine passed out of childhood, into the very beginnings of adolescence, certain that those decisions would last a lifetime. Her family still knew nothing of this part of her life.

When Catherine turned twelve, she was no longer allowed to go out on the streets alone, even to Mass. She was old enough to marry now. Her virtue had to be protected while her father and brothers sought a suitable husband for her, one who would bring them strong family connections.

Lapa urged her to bathe more often, and to curl and dye her hair. Catherine wanted no part of such self-indulgent vanity. She was not interested in marriage nor the effort to attract men.

Lapa did not understand. She reasoned that a woman's primary role in life was to marry and serve her husband. That was what she, Lapa, had done. That was what all her other daughters had done. That was what women were expected to do. She yearned to see her darling daughter suitably married and settled. Catherine was so precious to her mother, she of

15

the golden curls, the only baby out of twenty-five that Lapa ever nursed herself. She should have a good man, the best possible man, and take good care of him. Surely Catherine would see the wisdom of that plan in time. It was the only plan for a daughter. Lapa, believing she was doing it for Catherine's good, talked tirelessly about marriage and beautification.

The brothers, in the meantime, were looking for a suitor whose family could help them advance in the financial and social world of Siena. Endlessly they discussed desirable families: Did they have money? Did they have land? Where did they stand politically? What was their business? How many sons were there?

Catherine resisted the nagging of her mother and the pressures of her brothers. Months passed in a standoff; the strong-willed daughter against her strong-willed family. Still she never told them about her secret love for Jesus, or her visions, or her vows.

Buonaventura pleaded her parents' cause, and for a brief period Catherine agreed to make herself attractive, a decision she would regret till the end of her life. The priests who were her biographers give us few details of this time in Catherine's life. They probably did not understand the dictates of fashion or the temptations to vanity a young girl might feel when so much is being made of her appearance and her dress. Catherine agreed to dye and curl her hair and to wear pretty dresses. She went with her family to festivals and family parties where she met other young people.

Her family was greatly encouraged by this softening on Catherine's part. They soon found a suitable bachelor from a good family. But their hopes were dashed. Buonaventura died in childbirth, and Catherine dropped the grooming program immediately, vowing that she would never again indulge in such vain and frivolous behavior. She would not marry the young man her family had found or, for that matter, any other young man.

Catherine felt great remorse over her short flirtation with the world of fashion and frivolity. For the rest of her life the subject would come up in her confessions. Her confessors and biographers gave no indication of any sin on her part, but Raymond of Capua had harsh words for Buonaventura and the role she played. "The Lord," he wrote, "struck her down and made her pay the penalty of a painful death because she sought to draw aside to worldly things the heart of one who was bent on serving Him."[4]

Giacomo and Lapa and their sons were bewildered by Catherine's sudden reversal. They called in their old friend and nephew Tommaso della Fonte, who by now was ordained, to see if he could talk his cousin into being reasonable. Catherine was able to tell him the truth she had not been able to reveal to her parents: that she was already promised to Jesus and would never take another bridegroom.

Tommaso understood such a calling. He also understood Catherine's family. At his suggestion Catherine shaved her head, a traditional sign of a young woman's intention to become a nun and not a wife, a symbolic act no one would misunderstand.

Lapa did not misunderstand, but she also did not accept. When she discovered what Catherine had done to her beautiful golden curls, her shrieks could be heard blocks away.

The family embarked on a new strategy. If Catherine refused to marry and serve the husband they had chosen for her, very well, she could stay at home and serve her family.

The maid was dismissed and Catherine became the family maid. Her room was taken away from her, as was all time and space for privacy. She was forbidden to pray or to be alone where she could think about God.

Deprived of the privacy of her room for prayer, Catherine, like so many contemplatives before and after her, made a prayer cell within herself. Raymond of Capua tells us that "under the inspiration of the Holy Spirit" Catherine "began to build up in her mind a secret cell which she vowed she would never leave for anything in the world. She had begun by having a room in a house, which she could go out of and come into at will; now having made herself an inner cell which no one could take away from her, she had no need ever to come out of it again."[5] She could be in touch with God and aware of His presence no matter where she was or what she was doing.

Her family, especially her brothers, ridiculed her openly, taunting her as she served them. She ignored their jeers and did her chores cheerfully, even joyfully, pretending that she was serving the Holy Family in Nazareth: her father was Jesus, her mother was the Virgin Mary, and her brothers were the Apostles.

For many months Catherine lived this way, obeying every command of her family on the outside and communing with God on the inside. Then one night she had a dream in which she saw the founders of the great religious orders: Saint Benedict, Saint Romuald, Saint Bernardo Tolomei, Saint Francis, and many others. She searched for one — Saint Dominic, whose followers were important in the church of Siena. When she saw him, he stepped toward her and said, "Be of good heart, my daughter, and fear not! Assuredly thou shalt wear this habit."[6] He handed her the black-and-white habit of the Mantellate.

Encouraged by this dream, Catherine decided to tell her family her secret: "You must know then that when I was quite a little girl I made a vow of virginity to our Lord Jesus Christ, . . . and I promised Him that I would never marry anyone but Him through all eternity. So I advise you to throw all thoughts of an engagement for me to the winds because I have no intention whatsoever of obliging you in that respect: I must obey God rather than men. Further: if you want to keep me in this house as a servant I am quite prepared to stay and willingly do my best to serve you; but if you prefer to cast me out you can rest assured that I shall not deviate from my intention by a hair's breadth. I have a rich and powerful Husband who will never let me die of hunger, and I am certain that He will never let me go without any of the things I need.'"[7]

Giacomo heard and understood. He had long suspected that his daughter was acting with strength from beyond herself. He had even seen a kind of vision. One day when he was walking by Stephen's room, he saw Catherine stooping, as if she were making the bed. But she did not move. Giacomo watched for several minutes, but she made no motion at all. He thought she must be praying again, in spite of his instructions, and was about to rebuke her for such disobedience when suddenly a white dove appeared and hovered over her head. In an instant the dove was gone and so was Giacomo's anger. He left Catherine where she was, unsure about what he had seen or what it could mean.

Now that Catherine had spoken her truth, it became clear to her father that it was the Holy Spirit who strengthened and inspired her. "God forbid, darling daughter," he finally told Catherine, "that we should oppose the divine will from which it is clear your holy intention proceeds. . . . Keep your vow. Do exactly as you wish, and as the Holy Spirit teaches you. From now on we shall leave you in peace to your holy works, and put no more obstacles in the way of your holy exercises."

Then turning to the rest of his family, Giacomo said, "From now on let no one upset this my dearest daughter or dare to interfere with her; let her serve her Husband freely and pray to Him for us unceasingly. We could never find a relative in any way comparable to this One."[8]

2

The Years of Solitude

Giacomo Benincasa was as good as his word. He restrained his sons from interfering with their sister's decision to lead a celibate life. He hired a servant to relieve Catherine of all domestic responsibilities. Best of all, he gave her a room of her own where she could live and pray in privacy.

It was a small room, in the back of the house, near the kitchen, with one small window that opened onto the back alley. Catherine kept the window closed much of the time because of the stench from the alley. She kept the door closed, too, which made the room dark and stuffy. But it was Catherine's own, and she loved it.

With joyful anticipation she readied her room for her new life. First she hung a crucifix on the wall. Next to it, on a table, she put an oil lamp so the image of her Beloved would be visible night and day. A small chest in one corner held her few possessions, clothes mostly. Though she had no interest in appearance, Catherine liked to keep her body as clean as her soul. On top of her clothing she placed her scourge.

The only other furnishing was a couch. She covered it with planks and sat on it by day, or prostrated herself on it in prayer. At night it served as bed and mattress, as she lay upon it fully clothed. For a pillow she used a log.

The room that Catherine had wanted so desperately and for so long was a barren little hole-in-the-wall. It had the warmth and charm of a damp cave. It was exactly what Catherine wanted. In the darkness of this cell she opened her heart to her Beloved.

Often she addressed her prayers to the Father, but even as she spoke to Him, her mind and her eyes were fixed on His suffering Son. "O immeasurably tender love! Who would not be set afire with such love? What heart could keep from breaking? You, deep well of charity, it seems You are so madly in love with Your creatures that You could not live without us!" The words poured from her heart. "If I see clearly at all, supreme eternal Truth, it is I who am the thief, and You have been executed in my place. For I see the Word, Your Son, nailed to a cross. And You have made Him a bridge for me, as You have shown me, wretched servant that I am! My heart is breaking and yet cannot break for the hungry longing it has conceived for You!"[1]

Day and night Catherine knelt before the crucifix and gazed upon the wounds of Christ. She yearned to relieve His sufferings. She yearned to share His sufferings. As a bride yearns to become like her bridegroom, Catherine yearned to become like Jesus. As Jesus chose the pain of the cross in this life, so she chose pain and suffering.

Catherine was thirteen years old, living in a dark, stuffy cell, meditating on the crucifix hour after long hour. She could not read and so she could not study and meditate on other parts of the Gospel. She studied and meditated on what was available to her — the crucifix. Through the crucifix she came to know God's love for her, and she responded by loving Him with all the strength and intensity of her great heart. She chose to show her love by embarking on a life of voluntary pain.

She scourged herself three times a day, for an hour and a half each time, with a chain tipped with iron hooks. The hooks ripped open the flesh of her back, and the blood ran down her legs, forming pools on the floor. Catherine offered the pain for her own sins, for the sins of the living, and for the souls in purgatory.

She wore a hair shirt for a time; however, because she was fastidious about cleanliness, she replaced it with rough but washable woolen clothing and a thin iron chain fitted with tiny crosses. She wound the chain tight around her waist until the crosses dug in and cut her flesh.

She fasted. She had eaten no meat since early childhood. Now she gave up sweets, all rich food, and wine. Her meals, on the days she ate at all, consisted of bread and raw vegetables. Usually she took these meager meals alone in her room.

She deprived herself of sleep, the form of self-denial she found most difficult of all. Each night she forced herself to stay awake a little longer, keeping vigil with her Savior. In this way she reduced her sleep to a half hour every other day.

When Catherine began this program of self-denial and suffering, she was a strong, healthy girl. Her mother said she once could carry heavy sacks of grain from the cellar to the attic. But her self-torture left her thin and frail and kept her in pain for the rest of her life. Raymond of Capua wrote that few people could stand the pain that Catherine endured constantly.

Self-inflicted suffering of this sort was considered a normal part of the road to sanctity in fourteenth-century Italy. People who sought a close relationship with Jesus accepted the suffering that came to them, and added to it with fasting, scourging, use of hair shirts, and other forms of self-denial and self-punishment. Extreme suffering was considered a sign of holiness; something to be admired. The stories from Jacobus de Voragine's *The Golden Legend* glorified it.

The great saints of the region practiced this sort of spirituality. Saint Francis and Saint Clare did. (We will discuss these two saints of Assisi in a bit more detail in Chapter 11.) Francis eventually told his followers to throw out their hair shirts and scourges, but not until he had broken his own health with extreme fasting and self-punishment. Clare, too, insisted on moderation in penance for her followers, after she learned for herself the dangers of immoderation. Saint Dominic, Catherine's great spiritual mentor, used to scourge himself three times a day as Catherine did, and practiced other painful forms of penance. Unlike the saints from Assisi, Dominic recommended these practices to his followers.

Catherine's approach to suffering followed a pattern established by these saints who preceded her. She differed from their pattern, however, in two important ways: she was young and unsupervised. If she had chosen a cloistered life, the wisdom of her order and the discernment of her superior might have moderated her regime. If she had lived a normal life at home, her parents might have insisted that she temper her self-denial. But she did not enter a convent and she did not allow her parents to influence her. She arranged her life so that no one could stop her from expressing her love for Jesus by enduring pain. The love in her heart was enormous. So was her willingness to suffer.

We have no record of her father's reaction to her new way of life, but her mother hated it. Lapa, poor simple Lapa, did not understand or accept what her daughter was doing. Her husband had forbidden her to interfere with Catherine's chosen way, but Lapa still yearned to see her daughter married and having lots of happy, healthy babies. No decision of Giacomo's could change the horror Lapa felt when her own flesh and blood was mutilating herself. The sounds of the scourge were a torture to her.

Lapa tried repeatedly to make Catherine stop her penitential practices. She would insist that Catherine come and share her soft, warm bed, instead of keeping vigil on the hard cold boards. Catherine would obediently lie beside her mother in the luxurious feather bed, but as soon as her mother fell asleep she would slip away to her pallet and her prayer.

At Lapa's insistence they went to a fashionable spa where the warm healthful springs could soothe and heal the battered body. Her secret hope was that Catherine might develop a taste for luxury. The daughter was as wily as the mother. She agreed to go to the spa on the condition that she could bathe alone. Alone, then, she headed for the hottest part of the spa, the very source of the spring itself, where she nearly scalded herself to death.

"I thought about the pains of hell and purgatory," she told her mother, "and I asked my Creator to accept the pain I felt in the water in exchange for the pain in the next world which I know I deserve for my many sins."

Catherine and her mother were two strong-minded women, and they disagreed completely. Raymond of Capua believed that it was the devil himself who made Lapa try so hard to protect Catherine from pain. She was "stung by the Serpent in her maternal feelings," he wrote.

Lapa thought Satan was busy in someone else's life. When she heard the sound of the scourge striking the flesh she loved, she cried out so all the neighbors could hear, "Daughter, Daughter, I can see you dying before my very eyes! You'll kill yourself, of a truth you will. Oh, mercy me, who wants to take my daughter away? Who is bringing all these misfortunes upon me?"[2] She wept, she shrieked, she bullied, she tricked. But she did not change her daughter's mind.

Catherine longed to be understood by her mother. "I have desired to see you a true mother, not only of my body but of my soul," she cried.[3] But understanding did not come, and her mother's attitude became one more source of pain that Catherine accepted willingly for love of Christ crucified.

Catherine thought often of the dream in which Saint Dominic had given her the black-and-white robes of the Sisters of Penance of Saint Dominic, the Mantellate, as they were called. She yearned to wear those robes as a sign of the life she had chosen: black for humility, white for purity. But she did not meet the usual qualifications for that order. The Mantellate were Tertiaries, women who lived in the world, in their own homes, among their own family and possessions, and devoted themselves to prayer, penance, and the needs of the poor. Because its members were so visible and so loosely supervised, the Third Order of Saint Dominic insisted that its women be of impeccable character and respectability. Generally speaking, only widows, mature widows who would vow not to remarry, were admitted.

This was the order Catherine wanted to join. She begged her mother to get the Sisters' permission for her to enter. Reluctantly Lapa visited the Sisters and came home joyful with the news that the Mantellate never took girls as young as Catherine; moreover, the order never took virgins, only widows.

Catherine was not eligible, but neither was she discouraged. She believed that Saint Dominic, who had handed her the cloak and mantle in her dream, would overcome the regulations and customs of the Sisters.

A short time after Lapa's first visit to the Sisters, Catherine became seriously ill. Raymond described her illness as a disease that often attacks adolescents, and then suggested it was brought on by the hot water of the springs. He also admitted that he thought God had caused it. In any case, Catherine ran a high fever and broke out with ugly blisters all over her body. Her constitution, already seriously weakened by her fasting and penances, was in no condition to fight off any disease.

Lapa was sure "the sunshine of her life" was dying and became frantic. She promised God and Saint Dominic and all the other holy saints that she would do anything they asked if only they would save her daughter. Catherine, single-minded even at the point of death, told her mother that she should talk the Sisters into accepting her into their order. "If you don't," she warned, "I'm afraid that God and Saint Dominic between them will see to it that you don't have me with you in any kind of habit."[4]

This time Lapa got the Sisters to soften their position somewhat. They agreed to accept Catherine, provided she was not too pretty. "Come and see, and judge for yourselves," suggested Lapa. The Sisters came, and saw a very sick young girl whose face was blistered and peeling. They judged that as soon as she was recovered she could receive the mantle.

Catherine recovered fast, looking forward to wearing the black-and-white robe and mantle. But there was one more obstacle to overcome — the temptations of her own flesh.

Late one afternoon, shortly before she was to receive the habit, as she knelt in prayer she thought of her sister Buonaventura, and how happy she had been when her first child was born. Catherine realized, with a pang, that she would never know that happiness if she took the habit. Other memories, other pictures came to her: Buonaventura on her wedding day, smiling up at her new husband; a cousin picking up her beautiful little daughter and laughing for the sheer joy of being with her; lovers sneaking off from family gatherings hand-in-hand, excited to be alone together, even for a few minutes; women with their men; women with their children; happy, satisfied women.

In the failing light she heard a male voice ask, "Why did you cut off your golden curls?" When she did not reply, the speaker came closer. "Why do you wear a hair shirt next to your white body, and now, in a few days, the coarse habit of the Sisters? Look, is not this raiment much fairer?"[5]

A handsome young man stood before her offering her the most beautiful silken dress she had ever seen, embroidered with gold and pearls and jewels. Catherine was about to take the dress, when suddenly she realized what was happening. "No!" she cried, and she pushed the dress away. The tempter vanished. The temptation was resisted. But Catherine was left with a lot to think about.

She had been so consumed by her fight for the right to live as the bride of Christ that she had not taken time to consider other ways to live. She had fought so hard against her mother; she had never stopped to listen to what her mother was saying, that there were pleasures and comforts in marriage which were good and natural and satisfying. Her victories over her mother and father and the Mantellate seemed empty compared with the satisfactions of married life. She had won, but what had she won? The right to live in a bare, dark room? The right to suffer pain and loneliness all the days of her life?

Yes, she had won all of that, but much more besides. She had won the right to live for her Beloved, her Redeemer, to pray to Him, and to serve Him and to suffer for Him. Catherine turned away from thoughts of lost pleasure and threw herself at the feet of the crucifix, weeping: "O my only, my dearest Bridegroom, You know that I have never desired any but You! Come to my aid now, my Savior, strengthen and support me in this hour of trial!"

The image on the crucifix did not change. But Catherine heard the rustling of silk behind her. Turning she beheld the Blessed Virgin herself, carrying a glittering silken dress embroidered with gold and studded with pearls and precious stones. "My daughter," she said, "I have drawn this garment from the heart of my Son. It lay hidden in the wound in His side, as in a golden casket, and I have made it myself with my own holy hands." Then, as Catherine bent down, Mary clothed her in the heavenly garment she had chosen.

Once more Catherine had accepted Christ's special invitation to her; from the very depth of her maturing heart she had affirmed the "yes" she first spoke at the age of six. A few days later she went with her mother and father to a small side chapel of the great cathedral of San Domenico, where she received the black-and-white habit she longed for and the life that went with it.

Catherine believed that she had been called by Jesus and

Saint Dominic to live a holy life, symbolized by the black and white of the Dominican mantle, a life of innocence, purity, and humility, a life that rejected self-will and the desires of the flesh.

"Here you are then," she said to herself, "in the religious life. It is no longer right for you to live as you have been living. Your secular life is over now; the new religious life has begun and you must start living according to its rules."

The rules Catherine chose to live by were more stringent than those the Sisters of Penance of Saint Dominic asked of its members. Because they were a Third Order (that is, a lay, or secular, order), the Mantellate were not required to make the three great vows that nuns in religious orders make — the vows of chastity, poverty, and obedience. Catherine, nevertheless, made these vows herself, privately but solemnly. The Sisters were not required to live cloistered lives, but Catherine imitated the most austere cloistered life she could imagine.

She continued to live at home, in her cell, leaving it only to attend Mass. She imposed silence upon herself, speaking only in confession. She kept up her practices of prayer, fasting, and penances, intensifying each as she could. Her tiny meals became even tinier, and she made "an offering of tears to the Lord" with each. As before, she took "the discipline" three times a day, and she fought a constant battle with her body over the need for sleep.

For three years Catherine lived this intense life of self-denial, depriving herself of light and sound, sleep and nourishment, and applying both the chain and the scourge.

As her body weakened under this treatment, her spirit grew strong and healthy. Her confessor, Raymond of Capua, wrote, "There seemed to be two Catherines in her, one that suffered in a state of exhaustion, and another that toiled in the spirit; and the latter, fat and healthy of heart, sustained and strengthened the weakened flesh."[6]

It was Jesus who sustained and consoled her spirit during

this period of physical privation. She told her confessor she could almost always perceive Jesus' presence. At first He appeared in her imagination as she prayed. Later He appeared more and more often to her physical senses. She could actually hear His voice with her ears, and see His body with her eyes. Often He brought His Blessed Mother or some other heavenly guest. Though Catherine allowed no human companions into her cell, she was seldom alone. Jesus was her constant companion, teaching her the great truths about God, about sin, and about salvation.

"Father," she once told Raymond, "you can take it as certain that I have never learned anything about the way of salvation from men or women, but only from the Lord Jesus Christ, either in the form of inspiration, or through His speaking to me as I am speaking to you now, before your very eyes."[7]

Though Jesus was her constant Companion, He and His saints were not her only spiritual visitors. From time to time she was besieged by hordes of grotesque, howling demons. Some days she dreaded returning to her room after Mass because of the crowds she knew would be waiting for her there, screaming at her, drowning out all thought and prayer.

On one occasion the demonic visitors assaulted her mind and imagination with sexual feelings and desires. Catherine repelled them by turning her mind to prayer, but their howls and assaults made prayer difficult. They took bodily form, appearing before her as men and women engaged in sexual acts, both natural and unnatural. Catherine shut her eyes, but the visions continued. She scourged herself more than ever and prayed through the night so that she had no sleep at all. Still the hideous attack continued.

"Why do you go on punishing yourself like this to no purpose?" asked one apparition in a soft, loving voice. "What good can all this suffering do you? Do you think you can keep this up forever? You would kill yourself and then you will be a murderer. Better to stop now before you break down altogether. There is still time for you to enjoy yourself in the world — you are still young, and your body will soon again be healthy. Be like other women; get yourself a husband and have children and increase the human race."

This demonic attack continued day and night. Nothing Catherine tried could stop her tormenters for long. Coming back from church one morning, she had a sudden inspiration from the Holy Spirit. She remembered that the day before the attack began she had asked her Lord for the gift of fortitude and He had told her how to obtain it: "If you want to have the strength to overcome all the enemy's powers, take the cross as your refreshment."

Now she understood it all. Her loving Lord had allowed these temptations so she would understand the truth He had spoken to her. She could bear them cheerfully then, for as long as Jesus allowed them.

A particularly hideous demon sneered at her new attitude. "You wretched creature," he croaked, "do you intend to live this way for the rest of your life? If you do not give in to us we shall persecute you until the very day you die."

Full of faith, Catherine replied, "With joy I have chosen the way of suffering and shall endure these and any other persecutions in the name of the Savior for as long as it shall please Him to send them; in fact, I shall enjoy them."

With that, the demons dispersed and Jesus appeared to her for the first time since the attack began.

"My Lord," asked Catherine, "where were You when my heart was disturbed by all those temptations?"

"I was in your heart," came the reply.

"But how can I possibly believe that You were in my heart, Lord, when it was full of ugly, filthy creatures?"

"Did these thoughts and temptations bring content or sorrow, delight or displeasure, to your heart?" asked the Lord.

"The greatest sorrow and displeasure," said Catherine.

"Well, then," said the Lord, "who was it made you feel this displeasure if not I, who was hidden at the center of your heart? If I had not been there they would have entered your heart and you would have felt pleasure in them, but my presence there caused them to displease you."[8]

It had been a very painful lesson, but one Catherine never forgot: that Christ is present with us even when we do not feel His presence.

Most of Catherine's time was spent less dramatically. Day after day she had long, comfortable talks with the Lord, asking Him questions, receiving His instruction, learning to know Him, looking into His heart and seeing His great love for all His creatures, and His great suffering because of their sins.

Often as she prayed she was lifted up to heaven where she saw the saints and shared their life of bliss. At other times they visited her. On one occasion Jesus asked Mary Magdalene to take special charge of Catherine and act as her spiritual mother. Catherine developed a great devotion to the sinner-saint who had loved Jesus so well. She reported that after Jesus' ascension, the Magdalene had gone to live in a cave, praying, fasting, and doing other acts of penance for the rest of her life.

During this time of solitude and prayer Catherine began to wish she could read. She yearned to read the Holy Office, joining her prayers with those of priests, monks, Brothers, and Sisters throughout the Church. One of the Mantellate, Alessia Saracini, who came from a noble family in Siena and was educated, lent Catherine an alphabet book so she could learn the letters. Catherine applied herself to the task with her usual abandon, but to no avail. Even after weeks of study she could not distinguish one letter from another.

She cried out to her Bridegroom in her impatience, "If You want me to be able to read, You will have to teach me Yourself. If it is not Your will for me to read I will remain in my natural state of ignorance."[9]

From that moment, Catherine began to make progress and eventually was able to read fluently. Raymond of Capua reported, however, that although she was able to read and understand, she was never able to spell words out. The ability to write did not come to her with reading. For most of her life, her writing was done by dictation.

The ability to read changed the nature of Catherine's prayer. She told Raymond that Jesus often joined her and read the Holy Office with her, at which times she would have to change the words slightly, saying "Glory be to the Father, and to You, Lord, and to the Holy Spirit."

And so she lived for about three years, in what the world calls silence, with human voices and people blocked out, so she could concentrate on the voice of Christ. She subdued her body so it would not compete with the voice of her Beloved. She gave up everything for the sake of Jesus and on the night of Shrove Tuesday, 1367, she received a reward that exceeded her wildest expectations.

It was the last night of the carnival in Siena, a pre-Lenten celebration that Raymond called "the feast of the stomach," a time of wild parties and feasting, with music and dancing spilling out of the houses and into the streets. The sounds of revelry were everywhere in Siena. They even crept through the high hatch window into the dark cell where Catherine kept vigil before the crucifix.

As she prayed, Jesus appeared to her and said, "Since for love of me you have forsaken vanities and despised the pleasure of the flesh and fastened all the delights of your heart on me, now when the rest of the household are feasting and enjoying themselves, I have determined to celebrate the wedding feast of your soul and to espouse you to me in faith as I promised."

While He was speaking, His Blessed Mother entered the room, along with the Apostle John, Saint Paul, Saint Dominic, and King David with his harp. While David played sweet music, the Blessed Virgin took Catherine's hand in her own and presented the young virgin to her Son, Jesus, asking Him formally to marry Catherine to Himself in faith.

Jesus graciously accepted, then held up a gold ring with a sparkling diamond set in the midst of four pearls. He took Catherine's hand and set the ring on her second finger, saying, "There. I marry you to me in faith, to me, your Creator and Savior. Keep this faith unspotted until you come to me in heaven and celebrate the marriage that has no end. From this time forward, daughter, act firmly and decisively in everything that in my providence I shall ask you to do. Armed as you are with the strength of faith, you will overcome all your enemies and be happy."[10]

Jesus and the heavenly witnesses disappeared, leaving Catherine alone with the ring as proof of their visit. No one else ever saw the ring, but Catherine could always see it except, she admitted, blushing, when she had offended her heavenly Spouse and needed to go to confession. The ring constantly reassured Catherine of the special relationship she had with Jesus. She would need this reassurance in the years ahead.

3

The Handmaiden
of the Lord

Most bridal couples seek an idyllic spot, a place of rare beauty, to spend their first days and nights together. Catherine chose silence, solitude, and darkness. No earthly distractions would separate her from her Betrothed. In austerity Catherine was able to touch the living presence of Jesus.

She spent long leisurely hours every day with her Beloved. Sometimes they sang together, offering hymns of praise to their Father. Or they read the Holy Office, their hearts and minds united as they prayed the psalms. Most often they talked together, the Bridegroom telling the bride about His Father, His kingdom, His ways. The bride was an eager student whose quick mind hungered for knowledge of God. She listened and questioned, always seeking greater understanding of the profound truths He revealed to her.

After Communion, when they were physically present to one another in the Holy Sacrament, she would feel her soul leave her body. At such times she visited Jesus in His heavenly dwelling, reveling there in a beauty and a reality so extraordinary she could not describe it.

But the honeymoon was not to last. Like all honeymoons,

it was a preparation for the life to follow, and had to end so the next phase could begin.

One morning as Catherine sat with Jesus, He talked to her about the future and the work He wanted her to undertake. He reminded her that God asks two things of His faithful ones: love of God and love of neighbor. "I want you to fulfill both of these commandments," He told her. "I want you to walk in the way with both your feet. I want you to fly to heaven on two wings."

Loving God had been Catherine's sole occupation for years. She knew how to do that. But the thought of loving her neighbor was terrifying to her, even repulsive. For years she had suppressed all thoughts of humanity. She had shoved aside affection for other people for fear that they would become more important to her, even for a moment, than Jesus was. Her reasoning went something like this: God was holy, deserving of all her love. People were not holy. Now Jesus was telling her that she had to love them anyway. She did not know where to begin.

Yet deep within Catherine's heart there was a capacity to love people as well as she loved God. It was hidden from her, unused and unrecognized for many years. But it was not hidden from the eyes of Jesus.

"Do you remember when you were a little girl," He asked her, "how you felt such zeal for the salvation of souls?"

Catherine remembered. She remembered how exciting it was when Tommaso della Fonte read to her about the great preacher-saints who traveled to distant lands, spreading the Gospel and converting whole countries, saving thousands of people with their words. She remembered how she loved to hear about Saint Dominic fighting the heretics, teaching them the true faith; about how he fought selfish and sinful priests, urging them to reform their lives. He had always seemed like a hero to Catherine, a man of real courage, a man to emulate.

"Do you remember," Jesus asked her, "how you used to

dream of disguising yourself as a man so you could become a friar preacher and go off to teach my truth?" Catherine remembered that, too.

"I am now going to lead you on the path that will allow you to live out that calling which you have known since you were a little child," He told her.

Catherine was stunned by the idea. How could she, a woman, follow the path of Saint Dominic? Women did not walk on the streets alone. Women were not educated, except in domestic skills. Women's opinions were not respected when they spoke of "manly" affairs.

"I am but a woman and ignorant," she pleaded. "What can I do?" It was a human question and it received a divine answer.

"In my eyes there is neither male nor female, rich nor poor, but all are equal, for I can do all things with equal ease," said the Savior. "I spread abroad the grace of my spirit where I will."

He continued: "I realize that you do not speak from lack of faith but from humility. Therefore you must know that in these latter days there has been such an upsurge of pride, especially in the case of men who imagine themselves to be learned or wise, that my justice cannot endure them any longer. To confound their arrogance, I will raise up women, ignorant and frail by nature, but endowed with strength and divine wisdom. For it is only just that those who try to exalt themselves should be humbled. Therefore be brave and obedient when I send you out among people. Wherever you go I will not forsake you, I will be with you, as is my custom, and will guide you in all that you are to do."[1]

Thus Catherine was called to leave the security of her cell, her life of prayer and fasting, and to begin a new life, working with others, for the salvation of the Church. With great reluctance she accepted the mission. Rejoining the world was hard, but Jesus led her gently, one small step at a time, starting that very day. As the noon hour approached, He told her to join her family at their dinner table, something she had avoided for years.

Poor Catherine. It was easier for her to agree to reform the whole Church than to obey in this small matter. Jesus' words were like daggers stabbing at her heart. She did not want to leave Him. She had no desire for human company. She certainly had no desire for food.

But she had spent most of her youth learning to deny her own will so she could obey the will of God, and her training did not fail her now. She went upstairs to sit with her family as they ate.

When she entered the room, all conversation stopped. Men, women, and children stared as she walked around the table to sit near her mother. After a time the men turned their attention to their food once again, biting off great mouthfuls of bread and meat, gulping down huge draughts of wine. The only sounds in the room were the sounds of men chewing, swallowing, and smacking their lips as they ate. The women looked at their plates, unsure of what to say or do. Finally Lisa, the eldest of the Benincasa daughters-in-law, reached across the table and squeezed Catherine's hand. "I am so happy you are here!" she said. Catherine smiled. They all smiled. Conversation resumed around the table. Lapa urged Catherine to have something to eat, but she was not hungry. She sat quietly, watching, smiling, but as soon as the meal was over she hurried back to her room.

Being with her family had been a bewildering experience for her after her years of darkness and solitude. There were so many people, all moving and talking at once. She was dizzied by the sights and confused by the sounds. She found the smells of the rich food repulsive. But the most painful part of the ordeal had been facing her brothers, those overpowering young men who had ganged up on her so often and made fun of her desire to live apart. They had never understood her in the past

37

and they did not understand her now. Soon they would be joking at her expense again, sure that they had been right all along, that she could not take the celibate life.

This was a new kind of suffering for Catherine, but suffering is suffering, and she knew how to handle it. She accepted all the pain joyfully, grateful for the chance to suffer because Christ had suffered.

She joined her family at dinner every day after that. Sometimes she ate with them, but not often and not much. Instead she served as they ate. The servant role was familiar to her and she felt comfortable in it. She knew that she was being useful and that she was setting a good example for the others. That was always important to her. She wanted her family to see her living the way Jesus taught His followers to live. He told them to serve others, and Catherine was determined to do it.

With characteristic energy and enthusiasm, she took charge of the family kitchen, cooked all the food, served it, and cleaned up after the meals. She scrubbed and scoured till every pot and spoon was shiny. She assumed all the menial chores of the household. She did the family washing, going around in the dark of night to collect everyone's dirty clothes and washing them while the others slept. When the family's paid servant fell ill, Catherine took over her work and nursed the poor woman back to health as well.

Catherine spent little time socializing with her family. When she talked with them at all, it was about God. She loved to tell them, and anyone else who would listen, the wonders and glories that had been revealed to her.

There were many who wanted to listen. As Catherine made these first tentative moves out of her cell and into her family's life, guests at her father's table met her and were captivated.

Tommaso della Fonte, that steady old friend and cousin from her childhood, was still a frequent visitor. In fact, as her regular confessor, he was the only person she had spoken to for years. His devotion to Catherine was enormous. He was eager to listen to her and he brought along friends who listened, too. They were earnest young Dominicans, on fire with love of God. They came, according to the custom of the times, as her father's guests, but they stayed on as her followers and devoted friends.

Catherine poured out the knowledge and wisdom she had acquired in her little cell, and these young men drank it in and yearned for more. They recognized her as a greater teacher than any they had encountered in their seminaries, greater than any teacher they had ever hoped to meet.

One of these young men was Father Tommaso Caffarini, a scholar who taught at the University of Siena. He became an admirer who stayed with her through all the trials and triumphs of her life. After Catherine's death, his loyalty continued, as he spent years collecting reminiscences of those who knew her.

In one reminiscence Caffarini described how he himself felt when he was given some bread that she baked with her own hands. "I did not think it a little thing to have eaten it,"[2] he said. In fact, he did not eat all of it, but saved a piece to keep as a relic. He was aware, even in those early days, that he was in the presence of a remarkable saint.

Eating was a daily torture to her, he reported, because she was unable to digest solid food. Her parents insisted that she eat something at mealtime, and so she did, but vomited it all later. She came to think of family meals as "going to execution" because of the suffering they caused her.

Caffarini also wrote about the wounds with which she was often covered in those days; he said that she called them her roses and her flowers. They were the result of her self-scourging, "the discipline."

Another visitor, Father Bartholomew Dominic, wrote his recollections of those days: "When first I began to visit her, she was young, and her countenance was always serene and joyful. I was also young; yet, far from experiencing in her presence the embarrassment which I might have felt in the company of other women of her age, the longer I conversed with her, the more utterly were all earthly passions extinguished in my breast. I have known many — both laymen and religious — who experienced the same thing; there was something in her whole appearance so redolent of purity as to be far more angelic than human."[3]

It was exciting to be with Catherine, especially for idealistic young people who wanted to give their all to God. She knew so much about God and could talk about Him with such enthusiasm that they loved to listen to her. Her hatred of sin and love of God swept them all into a life of penance and purification none of them ever dreamed of.

Soon a small circle of followers had formed around her, young Dominican priests, some of the Mantellate, and Lisa whom Catherine called "my sister-in-law according to the flesh, but my dear sister in Christ." They met in her cell after supper most evenings, sitting on the very bench Catherine's heavenly visitors had used. "If only you knew who was sitting there earlier today," Catherine would say, and then she would go on to describe her prayer experiences and what she had learned from them.

Sometimes, when she talked of God in this way, she was lifted up in ecstasy. Her body became rigid, her eyes tightly shut. She could not see or hear anything, and if anyone touched her she could not feel it. One observer said she looked more like a statue than like a live human being. Her friends reported that at times they could see her body slowly rise toward the ceiling, remain there for a time, and then slowly descend again before she woke from her ecstatic state.

On other occasions she cried out in prayer, "O Inestimable Charity! O Eternal Truth! When shall I have the happiness of suffering something for Thy glory? Yet if in this desire Thou seest aught of vanity or self-love, I conjure Thee annihilate it, destroy it, tear it out of my heart!"[4]

Catherine found these ecstatic lapses embarrassing when they occurred in the presence of others. "I am not fit to converse with others," she told her confessor. "I entreat you, let me go elsewhere."[5]

But there was no "elsewhere" for Catherine anymore. She had lost the privacy of her cell where she could speak to her Lord and Savior in ways that she alone would know. She was a public person now, called to a mission in the world. A group of loyal friends had gathered around her. They would learn about every part of her life, including her most intimate conversations with God.

The evenings in Catherine's little room included more than teaching and ecstasy. The group sang together, prayed together, and shared their hopes and dreams together. They had a good time. They became friends, not just of Catherine, but also of one another.

They learned from Catherine, of course. She was their teacher and they were her disciples. But she also learned from them. She learned how to be a friend and how to have fun. She learned how to laugh and how to let people know she cared about them.

They took her out of the house for walks to a nearby chapel where they could all pray to the saints whose relics were there, or for walks into the fields to pick flowers and enjoy the beauty of God's creation. Often when they sat in Catherine's room at night, singing and praying together, the women would weave the flowers into wreaths or crosses, which the men would then deliver to people Catherine was praying for that day.

With the women of the group, the Mantellate, Catherine began to visit the needy and the sick. This was the special mission of their order. It would have been very hard for Catherine to make these visits alone because of the customs of the times and her own natural shyness and inexperience. But with the help of her friends she learned how to serve the poor and soon she was going off on her own, bringing help to the sick and the hungry. Her neighbors welcomed the sight of the tiny frail woman, wearing the black-and-white robes of the Dominicans, hurrying through the streets on her errands of mercy.

Catherine, of course, had nothing of her own to give away. She owned a change of clothing, a set of beads, a scourge, a chain, and a crucifix. Nothing that would help a hungry family. But in her father's house there was plenty. Too much, Catherine thought. She was horrified to see her family live with an abundance of this world's goods; it took their minds off the other, more permanent world. She often prayed to God to make her family poor. So it was a great pleasure for her to give away her family's possessions. Giacomo Benincasa instructed all members of his household to cooperate with his daughter's charitable activities, giving her whatever she wanted. But they resisted. They gave what they thought they could spare and then put locks on their closets.

Catherine's friends — Caffarini, Bartholomew Dominic, and others — loved to tell about how their saint served the poor. Many of their stories recount miracles; all of them show a woman of generous heart and enormous energy.

Several stories tell of miracles with wine. When she tapped her father's wine supply to give to the poor, all that she took, and more, was replaced. In one story a cask her father knew to be empty produced excellent wine for a whole season after Catherine drew from it to give away. In other stories Catherine multiplied loaves of bread when the need arose.

The most dramatic stories are those in which Jesus appeared to her disguised as a beggar. One day a beggar came seeking alms while she was in church praying. She had neither jewelry nor money to give to the beggar, so she removed the silver cross from her prayer beads and handed it over. That night Jesus appeared to her with the silver cross, now decorated with precious jewels, and told her that because she had been so generous to Him when He was a beggar, this jeweled cross would await her in heaven.

On another occasion Catherine saw a poor beggar asleep in the alley near her room. She got him a loaf of bread, but when she went out to give it to him, he told her that his real problem was not hunger but cold. He needed a cloak. She gave him hers, her own black Dominican mantle that was so important to her. The beggar turned out to be Jesus, and the reward for her generosity was that she never felt cold for the rest of her life.

Catherine served the sick as well as the poor. She especially sought out the dying, lavishing on them all the tender affection she longed to give Jesus Himself. Jesus, she knew, did not need her care and could not receive it from her. But she could prove her love for Him by caring for those who were most precious to Him, those who were most needy.

At that time in Siena there was a great hospital called Santa Maria della Scala (La Scala for short), founded and run as a monastery. Most cooking and nursing were done by religious Brothers and Sisters, supervised by priests who ministered to the spiritual needs of the patients. Here the sick and the aged of Siena received loving attention and the most skilled care available. Women like the Mantellate were encouraged to come and tend the terminally ill who needed extra attention and soothing.

Catherine became a regular visitor to La Scala, taking the most difficult cases, the patients with the worst tempers and most vicious tongues, whose sores gave off the worst stench.

One of her patients was a poor woman named Cecca, a leper with putrid sores all over her body. The hospital wanted to send her to a leper house where she would be left to die with the other destitute lepers. Catherine fought to keep her in the humane atmosphere of La Scala. She promised to provide Cecca with everything she needed and to care for her personally.

43

The hospital agreed and so did Cecca, so Catherine visited night and morning to fix her meals and dress her wounds.

Cecca was grateful at first; but the disease made her bitter, and soon she began to abuse her nurse verbally. If Catherine arrived a few minutes later than usual, Cecca would be waiting to criticize her. "So finally, here comes my lady, queen of Fontebranda," she would cry out. "What a gracious queen she is, spending day after day in the Friars' church! Were you there all morning, my lady, with your Friars? It seems as though you can never get enough of those Friars!"[6]

Catherine accepted this sort of talk without a murmur, but Cecca's abuse became a matter of town gossip. When Lapa heard about it, she was furious. She feared for Catherine's reputation, having ugly innuendos shouted out like that day after day for everyone to hear. She also feared for her daughter's health. "If you keep this up with this woman you will end up a leper yourself and that I could not stand!" she cried.

"Have no fear about that, Mother," Catherine replied. "What I do for this poor woman, I do for God. He would never let me suffer for it."

But soon white sores appeared on Catherine's hands, the first sign that the disease was attacking her. She continued to trust in God and to care for Cecca. When the old woman died, it was Catherine who washed her body, dressed it for burial, and then carried it to the grave. Catherine herself buried Cecca, saying the appointed prayers for the departed soul. When that last act of charity was completed, the leprous sores disappeared, leaving Catherine's hands whiter and more beautiful than ever.

Another of Catherine's patients was a short-tempered Mantellata named Andrea who had a putrid sore on her breast. Andrea began to hate the one who took such loving care of her, then started vicious rumors about Catherine that hurt her reputation throughout Siena and infuriated all who loved her, especially Lapa. Catherine responded to the lies with patience and trust, and eventually God acted on her behalf, allowing Andrea to see Catherine in a glorified state, basking in heavenly light. Andrea became a changed person after that, one of Catherine's greatest supporters, willing to tell everyone that the rumors she once started were all lies.

One day, soon after Andrea's change of heart, Catherine removed the dressing from Andrea's breast so she could clean the cancerous sore. She staggered back with revulsion. The stench from the wound gagged her. She fought off an impulse to vomit, not wanting to embarrass or offend Andrea. Catherine was furious with her body for behaving in this way. She would not allow it to rebel against her will. And so when she finished cleansing the wound, she took the bowl of putrid matter and drank it down. As she did, all sense of revulsion died within her.

She later told her confessor, Raymond of Capua, "Never since the day I was born did any food or drink I ever took afford me such sweetness and delight." She revealed that she had gone a step further, and pressed her face into the wound that had offended her so, and found that it was no longer putrid, but smelled sweet and fresh.

That night when she knelt in prayer, Jesus appeared to her and praised her for letting the ardor of her love overcome the reflexes and instincts of her body. Then He invited her to put her mouth to the wound in His side, the fountain of life itself. "Drink, daughter, from my side," He said, "and by that draught your soul shall become enraptured with such delight that your very body, which for my sake you have denied, shall be inundated with its overflowing goodness."[7]

Raymond saw this extraordinary episode as a turning point in Catherine's life. He said that when Catherine drank from our Savior's wound, her soul was so filled with grace that it overflowed into her body, which never needed food again. "Never afterwards does she or can she take bodily food in the ordinary way as she had been doing up till now."

Andrea was not the only patient whose life permanently affected Catherine's. There was in Siena a proud and critical Mantellata named Palmerina. She came from a wealthy and noble family in Siena, but she had given everything she owned to a hospital called La Casa della Misericordia. According to Raymond she had done many things well, but she had not conquered her pride and was obsessively jealous of Catherine.

Catherine went out of her way to be kind to her, but Palmerina responded by refusing her visits and spreading ugly lies about her throughout the city. Catherine, on the other hand, prayed for her sister Mantellata.

Raymond reported that God allowed Catherine to see the incredible beauty of Palmerina's soul and the effect of pride on it, dragging it down toward eternal damnation. This sight inspired Catherine to pray all the harder for her sister.

Palmerina became ill, but remained stonyhearted and resentful of Catherine, refusing even to see her. Her illness turned grave, and Catherine received a revelation that Palmerina was at the brink of death.

Catherine prayed the more fervently, pleading with God, "O my Lord, if You will not grant me the mercy I have asked for my sister, I shall not leave this spot alive."

Palmerina hung at the very brink of death for three days while Catherine, in another part of town, prayed for her soul. At the end of the three days the Lord sent "a light from on high to enlighten that agonizing soul." Palmerina saw her sin and repented of it. And when Catherine tried to visit her one last time, the ailing Mantellata received her joyfully and then died with "great contrition of heart."

After Palmerina's death Jesus spoke to Catherine about the beauty of the soul He had allowed her to see. "I have shown you this soul that you may burn ever more ardently to procure the salvation of all souls, and induce others to do the same," He told her, and then He gave her a new gift. "I give your soul a special illumination which will enable you to see the beauty or ugliness of all the souls who come to you, so that your spiritual senses will henceforth perceive spiritual conditions, and not only of the souls present before your eyes, but of all whose salvation you ardently long for and fervently pray for, even though you have never seen them."[8]

This ability to see souls became an important part of Catherine's life, the foundation on which her friendships were built. She told Raymond, "I hardly ever notice anything of the physical movements of people around me. I am so engrossed in reading their souls that I don't pay attention to their bodies."

During this period of Catherine's life, when she was spending much of her time helping the poor and the sick, her immediate family needed her, too. In the summer of 1368, when she was twenty-one, her father became seriously ill. Catherine rushed to his side and stayed with him day and night, nursing him and praying for his swift recovery. But the Lord revealed to her that her father would not recover from this illness.

She talked to her father, then, about his approaching death, and asked him if he was ready to leave this life. He assured her that he was. Trusting in God's great mercy and the loving prayers of his daughter, he was ready.

Catherine continued to pray for him, asking her Bridegroom to allow her father to pass directly from this life into the heavenly kingdom. It was revealed to her that although her father's many virtuous deeds had won for him a place in heaven, still his soul had contracted some rust, and justice demanded that it be purified in the fires of purgatory.

The loving daughter pleaded, "Lord, how can I abide the thought that the soul of my dear father who nourished me and brought me up should go forth to suffer in the flames of purgatory? If Your justice must have its course, I beg You to turn it on me, and whatever pains are appointed for my father, lay the same on me and I will willingly bear them."

"Daughter," responded the Lord, "I am content that it

be so; therefore the pains due to your father I lay on you, to bear in your body even to life's end."[9] Later, after Giacomo died, Catherine was granted a vision of him in heavenly bliss. She cherished that memory as she suffered his pain which was added to the ongoing agony that wracked her body regularly.

Shortly after Giacomo's death, Lapa, too, became gravely ill. Again Catherine began to nurse her sick parent and pray for her recovery, and again she received a revelation that this was a terminal illness. But Lapa was not like her husband. No one ever accused her of living with one foot in heaven. The spiritual world that was so important to Catherine and her father was not very vivid to Lapa. She knew about this life, and she liked it, and she was not ready to leave it.

When Catherine talked to her about her approaching death, and how she should begin to prepare for it, Lapa, outraged, cried out: "You should be praying for my recovery, not my entrance into heaven!"

Catherine heard God say that many tragedies lay ahead if Lapa survived, but still her mother insisted that she wanted life, not death. She would not prepare herself for death in any way. Catherine begged God not to let her mother die unprepared. God could refuse Catherine nothing, it seemed. Lapa recovered. She lived to see plague, drought, and civil war come to Siena. She lived to bury most of her children and many of her grandchildren. In her old age she complained that God must have riveted her soul into her body, and now it could not escape and let her die like a natural woman. She often regretted that she had not left this life when she had the chance.

But in the end it was Catherine who won. Her mother overcame her fear of death, finally. She became more interested in the spiritual world, especially after so many near relations had departed. Lapa even joined the Mantellate before she died, giving her life over to prayer and penance and to acts of charity for the salvation of souls.

4

Catherine in a Man's World

A noisy band of men milled about the street near the well of Fontebranda. They belonged to a political faction that had just seized control of the city government and they were celebrating their new power. One of them spotted a member of the ousted party scurrying along a back alley, trying to reach the safety of his home. With a shout, the mob ran after him, and when they caught him, they played with him, as a cat plays with a mouse. They jeered him, spat on him, and tossed him about from one to another. After a while they tired of him and kicked him into insensibility, then went off in search of another victim.

The sounds of the mob could be heard in the Benincasa house, where Catherine sat with her brothers and their families. The cries grew fainter; the mob was moving away from the house. Perhaps they would not come for the brothers after all. But that seemed too much to hope for. The Benincasa brothers had been prominent supporters of the recently toppled "Party of the Twelve." This crowd would not forget or forgive any of their opponents. Forgiveness was not their way, it was not Siena's way. Blood feuds and death were the way disputes were settled in Siena.

Suddenly there was a loud banging at the door. "Open up! Open up!" cried a familiar voice. "It's me, Bartolo! Let me in!" Stephen opened to his friend and bolted the door again.

"You must flee!" gasped Bartolo. "Right now, while there is time. Go to the Church of Saint Anthony. The others are there. It is a refuge!"

"No!" It was Catherine who spoke. She had been sitting, praying silently for some time. Now she stood and spoke with quiet authority. "My brothers will not go to Saint Anthony's, and I feel sorry for anyone who does," she said.

Bartolo did not stay to argue. There were other families to warn, others who would welcome the news that a refuge had been found.

As soon as he left, Catherine put on her mantle and said to her brothers, "Do not be afraid now. Come with me, and walk bravely, like manly men."

With a brother on each arm, and a third walking just behind, Catherine made her way down the street, past the well, straight toward the milling crowd that stood between her and her destination on the other side of town. The men grew quiet as she and her brothers approached so boldly. Someone recognized two of the brothers and shouted, urging the mob to attack. But no one moved. They had also recognized the tiny Mantellata walking between her brothers.

Some had seen her bring food to a neighbor; some remembered hard times when she brought food to their own houses. Others knew her because she had nursed a relative in the hospital or cured someone they loved. They all knew her. She was a holy woman, their holy woman, *La Beata Popolana*. They bowed and backed away, leaving a clear path for her and her brothers.

Catherine escorted her brothers in safety to the hospital of Santa Maria della Scala where she asked the master of the hospital to keep Stephen and the others for three days, at which time she said it would be safe for them to be on the streets again. The master agreed, and so the Benincasa brothers survived the overthrow of the "Party of the Twelve," though many of their friends and political allies were massacred in Saint Anthony's Church.

Though their lives were saved, their fortunes were not. Without the cooperation of city officials the brothers could not make a profit in the dye business and within two years they left Siena altogether to start anew in Florence.

This change in status made little difference to Catherine. If anything, she was relieved that the dangers of wealth had been removed from her family's life. She spent her days as before, interrupting her prayers only to perform acts of charity and to welcome her friends who wanted to learn more about God.

For Lapa, however, the change was devastating. She stayed on in the house Giacomo had built for her many years before, but it was not the same with everyone gone. There were no servant girls left to bring her the news of the neighborhood; no young apprentices to worry over. More than anything else she missed her grandchildren. There were no healthy boys running up the stairs, breaking her eardrums with their shouts; no little girls to dress up in pretty clothes; no bouncing babies to hug.

There was no one left but Catherine, *La Beata Popolana*. Lapa was proud of her daughter, of course, but she did not feel comfortable around her. She was glad that Catherine was holy, but she longed for someone who would chat with her over a cup of tea. Catherine's talk about God and His infinite mercy was exciting to Father Dominic and the others, but not to Lapa. She liked a bit of gossip, and someone to fuss over. Catherine provided neither. Lapa sighed, "Life is nothing but a burden to me. I should have died when I had the chance."

Catherine did not enjoy her mother's company either. She could not take the place of all the people her mother missed; she could not fill the emptiness of her mother's life. She hated her mother's hunger for talk, her quest for news of the neighborhood, her interest in idle chatter. Catherine began to spend a lot of time away from home, sometimes at convents, sometimes at the home of Alessia Saracini, the Mantellata who once lent her an alphabet book and later became her great friend and confidante. There was always room for Catherine at Alessia's.

The big house near the Fontebranda remained Catherine's official home, but the little room below the kitchen was no longer her favorite place. She had learned to meet Jesus out in the wide world and to serve Him there.

The ways she served Him began to change, too. The traditional charitable works for women — caring for the poor and the sick — remained part of her life. But she began to find herself involved in other kinds of work for God.

One day when she was at Alessia's house, her prayers were interrupted by curses and shouts coming from a noisy crowd out in the street. People had gathered to watch two criminals being paraded through town on the way to their execution. They were notorious men, known throughout the region for their hard hearts and cruel deeds. As they rode past in their tumbrel (a cart especially made for prisoners), the men were pinched with red hot tongs. Shrieking in pain, the condemned men cursed God and all the saints. The bystanders hooted and jeered.

When Catherine saw what was happening, she began to intercede for the men. "I know that these men are justly punished for their offenses," she prayed. "But so was the thief who hung next to You on the cross, and You took pity on him, promising that You would see him that day in paradise. Look down now on these wretched creatures, and soften their hearts so they may be spared from the second death."[1]

Raymond tells us that in response to this prayer God allowed Catherine to accompany these men "in the spirit" on their terrible journey, weeping and praying for them along the route. According to Raymond, demons traveled the route, too, laughing and gloating over the victory that would soon be theirs, and howling with anger at Catherine's interference.

When they came to the gate where the execution was to take place, in answer to Catherine's prayers Jesus appeared to the two criminals, looking the way He did on His own execution day, with His hands bound, blood and sweat running into His eyes, and more blood flowing from the wounds on His back. He looked into the eyes of the two tortured men, and their hearts were touched. They saw themselves as they really were, and they wept and asked to see a priest before they died. Many in the crowd that had accompanied the criminals all the way, hearing their curses and blasphemies, were astounded. They stood silent and awed as the men confessed their sins and went to their execution joyfully, like people going to a wedding.

The priest who heard their confessions told Father Tommaso della Fonte about the conversion of these notorious men, and he, in turn, ran to tell Catherine and Alessia. But they already knew. Catherine had seen it all, "in the spirit," and had ended her prayer for them with a happy sigh. "This day they will be with You in paradise, Lord," she said at the very hour of their execution.

News of the last-minute conversion of these notorious men spread far and fast; news of Catherine's prayer for them spread, too. She began to get a reputation as one who could work miracles with the hardhearted.

One such hardhearted individual lived in Siena, a young man named Andrea de' Bellanti who was the despair of his parents because of his drinking and gambling and blaspheming. When he drank, he gambled and lost, and then he blasphemed, blaming God for his losses. Once, after a long night of drinking and losing at the gambling table, he entered a church, seized a painting of the crucifixion, and thrust his dagger through it over and over. On another occasion he stomped on a crucifix and burned a picture of our Blessed Lady.

When Andrea was just twenty years old, he was stricken with a mortal illness, but even this sickness did not change his attitude toward God. He became more hardened and bitter. His parents pleaded with him, and his parish priest visited him, but Andrea drove them away with curses. Father Tommaso della Fonte pleaded with him and prayed for him, but failed to soften Andrea's heart. Tired and discouraged after his unsuccessful vigil, Father Tommaso stopped at Catherine's house to ask for her prayers before he headed for home.

When Catherine heard the story, she began at once to beg the Lord to spare the soul He had created. "Lord," she cried, "if You look narrowly at our iniquities, who will be able to stand? Why did You come down from heaven and into the world? Why did You take on the holy and pure flesh of the Virgin Mary? Was it to call men to a rigorous account of their sins? Did You not come to take away men's sins, and lead them to Your mercy? O Lord, grant that my brother's heart may be softened and made to yield to the workings of Your Holy Spirit."[2]

Catherine prayed this way throughout the long night hours, and as dawn broke over Siena she heard the Lord promise all she asked. "Dear daughter, I can no longer resist you in this matter. Your tears and prayers have prevailed. I shall put away my sword of justice. This sinful man shall find the grace and favor you have sought for him."

As the sun peeped through the windows of Andrea's bedroom that morning, Andrea asked to see a priest. His wife could not believe her ears. "What is this you ask for?" she demanded. "I ask for a priest," was his reply. He said that he could see Jesus standing in the corner of his room, and Catherine standing with Him, demanding that he go to confession.

The story spread throughout the city: Andrea de' Bellanti died repentant, having received the sacraments. When Father Tommaso went to bring the good news to Catherine, she again knew more of the events of the morning than he did. Though she had never known Andrea or visited his house, she was able to describe him and his room in detail.

Catherine's reputation continued to grow in Siena. Mothers who worried about their sons asked for her prayers. Families caught in blood feuds sought her help. "When she talks to God, He listens," people said. When they wanted to be sure He heard their cases, they asked Catherine to talk for them. The results were spectacular. Sin-hardened old men softened and repented when she prayed for them. Defiant young men, too, responded to the grace God sent when Catherine interceded. Everyone in Siena heard stories about the holy woman from Fontebranda and her miracles.

But not everyone was impressed with the stories, or with Catherine. Father Lazzarino of Pisa was not impressed. He was a Franciscan who taught philosophy at the University of Siena, an intellectual who criticized Catherine's teaching publicly though he had never met her or heard her teach. Father Bartholomew Dominic, who also taught at the university, believed that pride led the Franciscan intellectual to be overly critical of Catherine, and he was greatly encouraged when Lazzarino wanted to meet her. On the appointed evening he and Father Tommaso brought the famous professor to Catherine's little cell, where she welcomed them graciously.

Father Lazzarino seated himself on the chest. Catherine sat near him on the floor. The others stood and listened to their conversation, which Father Dominic later wrote down.

After an awkward silence, Father Lazzarino opened the interview. "I have heard many persons speak of your sanctity," he said, "and of the great understanding which God has given you of the holy Scriptures; I wished to come to see you, hoping to hear something that would be of edification to my soul."[3]

Catherine responded with equal politeness and humility, saying, "And I, too, rejoice to see you, for I think our Lord must have intended to give me an opportunity of profiting by that learning with which you daily instruct your disciples. I hoped that you might be led out of charity to help my poor soul, and I beg you to do so for the love of God."

The conversation continued in this way, with more formality than substance, until it was time for the priests to leave. Then Catherine knelt before Lazzarino and asked for his blessing, which he gave with a grand gesture. Catherine rose, thanked the scholar, and asked him please to pray for her immortal soul. He agreed to, and, as a matter of courtesy, asked that she do the same for him. He left the house thinking that she was a good woman, but in no way extraordinary. It never occurred to him that her prayers might have a real effect on his life.

But the next evening when he sat down to prepare for his morning classes, he began to weep uncontrollably and without reason as far as he knew. In the morning when his servant came to wake him, he was still weeping. He could not teach. He could not appear in public. He could not rest. He could only weep.

As the day wore on he became exhausted, confused, and, for the first time in many years, humble. He got down on his knees and begged God to have mercy on him. If there was a sin on his conscience that was causing these incessant tears, he wanted to see it so he could make amends. He heard the quiet voice of God speaking to his heart, "Have you forgotten how you judged my servant Catherine in a spirit of pride, and asked her to pray for you out of formal politeness?" Lazzarino recognized the truth and repented.

At the break of dawn he hurried to Catherine's house and prostrated himself before her in humility. She, too, prostrated herself. Then the two sat side by side and talked and listened. Catherine already knew about Lazzarino's weeping and what caused it, as well as what cured it. "The way of salvation for you is to despise the vanities and applause of the world," she told him, "and to become poor, humble, and despised, after the pattern of Jesus Christ and your holy father, Saint Francis."

Lazzarino did exactly as she instructed him. He sold all his belongings, even his books, and lived a life of strictest poverty as Saint Francis had. He became a faithful disciple of Catherine from that day and was so changed in his attitude toward her that his worldly friends said he was "be-Catherined."

The Franciscan scholar was not the only man in Siena who was "be-Catherined." Catherine had entered the world of men and she dazzled them. The shy adolescent had matured into a woman who was comfortable with men, and they with her. There was nothing in the dangerous manly world of Siena that was too much for her: not the torture of criminals, nor the blasphemy of sinners — not even the pride of intellectuals. Catherine had become the kind of person she always urged her brothers to be: "a manly man." The men loved her for it and sought her out. Great men and lowly men enjoyed her company.

Other women in Siena did not live the way Catherine did, entering the world of men and talking to them as equals. Women served men, as Lapa did so well and so happily, by running their households and bearing their children. Any activity that took a woman outside her own house was suspect. Young girls who were marriageable were never allowed outside unchaperoned. Older women went out, but usually in the company of someone else, and only for certain purposes. A trip to church was considered acceptable, for instance, or a trip to buy groceries, or a visit to the sick or the needy. Unless a woman had one of these few specific reasons to leave the house, she was expected to be at home, tending her house, serving her husband.

Catherine grew up with these restrictions and accepted them, as other women did, without even giving them much thought. When Christ called her out of her cell to serve Him in the world, her first reaction was, "I cannot do that; I am a woman." But Jesus did not accept the restrictions. "In me there is no male or female," He told her. As the months and years went by, He led her step-by-step to a new way of living, in which a woman could come and go from her house with the same freedom as a man, in which she could talk to a man as an equal, and even discuss "manly" subjects.

"I care more about the opinion of my Heavenly Spouse," she declared, "than I do about the opinions of mere created beings." She took Jesus as her model, serving in many of the ways He did, teaching and counseling her followers as well as serving them food and waiting on them while they ate. She came and went from her house according to Jesus' instructions, rather than the conventions of the day.

She went to the hospital of Santa Maria della Scala often, especially at night, when the old and the dying were often frightened and needed comfort. Few citizens of Siena ventured out into the streets after dark. But Catherine did. She carried a lantern to light her way through the dark streets at night. She was such a frequent visitor to La Scala that a small room there was reserved for her so she could rest or pray whenever she needed.

Beneath the hospital was a series of vaults, or catacombs, where early Christians prayed secretly. When the hospital was built on the site in A.D. 832, the catacombs were preserved, and continued to be used as the secret meeting place of a group of pious men who called themselves "The Company of the Disciples of the Virgin Mary, Under the Hospital."

In Catherine's day these disciples wore penitential garb, met regularly to take "the discipline" (self-scourging), and observed Fridays and major feast days with long periods of prayer and meditation followed by celebration of Mass and reception of the sacraments. The men in this society were the spiritual elite of Siena, the most fervent seekers after truth. They were priests and scholars from the University of Siena, doctors and administrators from the hospitals. They were humble men in high places, and they recognized Catherine as a fellow seeker. They admitted her to their company and accepted her as their leader.

The company included Messer Matteo di Cenni di Fazio, who ran Misericordia Hospital; Fathers Tommaso della Fonte and Tommaso Caffarini, both of whom had served as Catherine's confessors and confidantes; two Augustinian monk-scholars; and Father Bartholomew Dominic, who served as Catherine's confessor when the two Tommasos were out of town and who wrote some of the most vivid accounts we have of Catherine's life. When Father Raymond of Capua was sent by his Dominican superiors to teach in Siena, he, too, joined the company.

Catherine was twenty-four years old and had never received formal schooling, yet these scholarly men called her "Mother" and "dearest Mama," and accepted her spiritual direction. Even her confessors considered themselves her spiritual sons; she obeyed them and accepted the direction they gave in confession, while they likewise obeyed her and accepted her direction.

"People often said that it was from the friars that she learned her wonderful doctrine," Raymond of Capua reported, "but the contrary was the case; it was they who learned from her."

The question of how Catherine acquired her knowledge of God and Scripture became a subject of great controversy. Many intellectuals in the Church could not believe that an unschooled girl had received what the Church called "infused knowledge." They assumed she was lying and practicing clever deceits. They wondered who was helping her with these deceits. "Could it be Satan?" they wondered. Vicious rumors circulated.

"The strife of tongues" is the way one biographer describes this period of the saint's life. It was not just the tongues of the intellectuals that were striving against her either. Among the common people there had often been ugly rumors. People questioned her virginity and why she spent so much time with monks and priests. Many were bewildered by her prolonged fasting. They doubted it was real. Perhaps she was eating in secret, they thought, or being fed by an incubus of Satan while she slept.

Within the Church itself, and even among the Dominicans of Siena, her way of life was by no means universally accepted. The frequency with which she came to receive Holy Communion (almost daily) was another subject of controversy. The accepted belief at the time was that frequent reception of the Holy Sacrament would make the worshiper less reverent. This clearly was not happening with her, yet bishops and priests often cited that policy and refused her Communion.

The Dominicans who served at the great cathedral in Siena had their own special problems with Catherine. When she approached the Communion rail, she wept and cried aloud. This fervor distracted other worshipers. Then after Communion her ecstasies provided another distraction, drawing the curious to the church and disrupting worship. The ecstasies might last for hours, even past closing time for the Church. More than once the church staff threw Catherine out into the street rather than keep the church open till she returned to herself.

Catherine accepted all these troubles, assuming they were sent by Jesus for her strengthening and instruction. If a bishop said that frequent reception of the Eucharist could lead a person to be less respectful of the gift, she thanked him for his fatherly concern and searched her soul for signs of disrespect. If someone told her that her continued fasting was the work of Satan and that she should pray to be released from his grip, she thanked the person for such wise counsel and begged him to join her in that prayer. Catherine's friends became angry and impatient with this continual criticism of their "dearest

Mama." But Catherine kept her patience and her gentle manners, and more often than not her accusers repented of judging her uncharitably.

Still, the rumors and controversy persisted. As Catherine appeared more often in public, and as her fame grew, the rumors grew more vicious.

Responsible people within the Church and within the Order of Preachers (Dominicans) believed there were serious questions that needed to be answered if Catherine was to continue this very public life. The most important questions dealt with her fasting and her knowledge of God. Were these gifts of God or the work of Satan?

In the spring of 1374 Catherine was summoned by the master-general of the Order of Preachers to appear before the general chapter in Florence. No record remains of what happened at that historic meeting. But she returned home without censure, and almost immediately Father Raymond of Capua, a scholar of great ability and renown, was sent to Siena to be her confessor and spiritual director.

Catherine had outgrown the abilities of Father Tommaso della Fonte and Father Tommaso Caffarini. They loved her and remained her friends, but they lacked the education and experience that Raymond could bring to the task of advising Catherine.

Years later, when Raymond wrote the official biography of Catherine, he said that her earlier spiritual directors had not understood her need to fast and had almost killed her by insisting that she try to eat. No other official criticism was made of them, though it is easy to believe that della Fonte, poorly educated like so many priests of his day, could not grasp the theological insights Catherine received in prayer.

Raymond, on the other hand, was a man of stature in the Church. Born of a rich and noble family, he was well educated and well traveled, a man of the world. He was also a mature man, seventeen years older than Catherine. He would not be overwhelmed by her revelations as young Father Tommaso della Fonte was.

When the Dominicans decided to send Raymond of Capua to Siena to be Catherine's confessor, they were sending the best man they had. Raymond's presence in her life gave her credibility in the larger Church outside of Siena. The result of the general chapter in Florence was not to silence Catherine, or denounce her as a heretic, but to raise her up in the eyes of all the Church as a holy person and great worker of miracles.

5

Maid of Tuscany

Catherine and her friends laughed and sang as they made their way along the dusty road from Florence to Siena in the warm June sun. They could not wait to get home to tell their families and friends all the wonderful things that happened in Florence. They had seen the great city on the Arno, with its Duomo and its Ponte Vecchio. They had made new friends, rich and influential men in the city and in the Church who loved Catherine and understood her, who stood by her when she needed them. Catherine had seen her brothers and their children. Ah, their children! What beautiful children! Catherine could have hugged them till her arms fell off.

But, best of all, Catherine had won the approval of the general chapter of the Dominicans. She had won! She had passed their test! The great scholars and theologians of her order questioned her for hours. They asked about her fasting and her penances, and about her doctrine and how she acquired it. They asked her to interpret passages of Scripture and explain key points in theology.

They were not trying to trick her, like some theologians she had met, just trying to understand her. They asked hard questions, but they listened carefully to her answers. And in the end they concluded what her friends had known all along:

that Catherine was a holy woman given exceptional graces and powers by God. They declared that it was safe for her to teach and preach publicly and they encouraged her to continue to follow promptings of the Holy Spirit.

The little group of friends hurried toward Siena, bursting with the news of Catherine's triumph. As they approached the city gate, they had to move to the side of the road to make way for a huge wagon leaving the city. They looked inside, as it passed, and to their horror they saw that it was filled with dead bodies, their faces blue, their stomachs bloated. The Black Death had returned to Siena.

There was no time for celebrating Catherine's victory, only time for work — visiting the sick, preparing them for death, and burying them. The rich had fled the city. Only the poor were left, and the dying, and those who worked with them.

The plague struck Catherine's family, among them her brother Stephen, her sister Lisa, and eight of her nieces and nephews. She nursed them and comforted them, and when they died, she bathed, dressed, and buried them with her own hands.

The Black Death killed off a third of the populace of Siena that summer. The smell of death and the shrieks of the dying filled the city. Wagonloads of dead were buried in mass graves outside the city walls. City services were discontinued because there were not enough workers. Crops were abandoned in the fields. In the convents and monasteries, too, the epidemic took its toll. Every quarter of the city, every family, every occupation was devastated by the plague in that summer of 1374.

During those awful weeks, Catherine worked day and night to comfort the dying and to help the others cling to life. Father Raymond of Capua worked, too. He had just arrived in Siena, assigned by his superiors to teach in the university so he could be near Catherine. All the priests of Siena were pressed into service, hearing the confessions of the dying and administering the last sacraments. Father Bartholomew Dominic worked with the dying; so did Fra Santi the hermit, and Messer Matteo de Cenni di Fazio, and the other members of Catherine's circle of intimates. Still there were never enough priests to answer all the calls of the dying.

Raymond said he hardly had time to eat or sleep because he received so many urgent messages from people who needed a priest right away. One morning when he tried to get up after just a few hours' sleep, he felt the telltale symptoms himself: a slight pain and swelling in his groin, followed by a fever and headache. At dawn, with help from a brother Dominican, he struggled to Catherine's house, only to learn she had not yet returned from her nightly rounds. Raymond, delirious by now, lay on a cot to wait for her.

When Catherine found him, she put her hands on his head and began to pray. She prayed for half an hour and as she did, Raymond could feel the symptoms weaken and recede as health and vigor filled his body. "It was as if something was being pulled out of me at the ends of all my limbs," he wrote. When Catherine stopped praying, he was completely cured. "Have something to eat now," she told him, "and then rest for a while and then go out again and work for the salvation of souls and give thanks to the Highest Who has saved you."[1]

Fra Santi, too, was struck by the plague. Catherine found him dying in his hermitage and had him moved to Misericordia Hospital, where he could receive loving care. She whispered to him, "Do not be afraid no matter how bad you feel. You are not going to die this time." When she came back to check on him a few hours later, he was in a coma. Again she whispered in his ear, "Do not be afraid; you are not going to die." Days went by and the condition of the holy hermit worsened; his friends gave up all hope. Catherine visited again and this time she shouted into his ear, "I command you, in the name of our Lord Jesus Christ, not to die!" At that, his spirit returned to his body, then he sat up in bed and asked for something to eat.[2]

The most famous of Catherine's Black Death miracles, and one depicted in a painting by G. del Pacchia, was the cure of Messer Matteo di Cenni de Fazio, rector of the Casa della Misericordia. Like so many others, he caught the plague working with the sick in his own hospital. It raged through his exhausted body. He felt the first symptoms at Mass one morning, and before the final prayer was said he was carried from the church like a dead man and brought to his room in the hospital. The physician who attended him told Raymond that there was no hope of his recovery.

Catherine received the news that morning when she got home from her nightly rounds. She set out immediately for Misericordia, and as she strode down the corridor toward her friend's room she cried out in a loud voice, "Out of bed, Messer Matteo, out of bed, out of bed. This is no time for you to be lying here taking your ease." Messer Matteo smiled when he heard that familiar voice and obeyed it. He got up, cured, and went back to work.[3]

At the end of summer the plague subsided, and life returned to normal, or as close to normal as possible in a city where so many had died. Catherine was suffering from extreme exhaustion, so she and Alessia and some of the other Mantellate went to the Dominican convent at Montepulciano to spend a few days resting and recuperating. Father Raymond went with them. He was familiar with the convent, having spent nearly a year there writing the life of Saint Agnes of Montepulciano.

At last Catherine and Raymond had a chance to get to know each other. They had labored side by side during the awful summer weeks. Now they had time to walk together in the cool fall days and enjoy the breathtaking Etruscan countryside.

Catherine had never met anyone like Raymond: intelligent, educated, confident of himself and of God. She loved and trusted him from the start. What is more important, perhaps, she trusted herself under his direction. Her intelligence and her spiritual insight had overwhelmed Father Tommaso della Fonte; he had never really given her spiritual direction; he had not even understood her. Raymond could understand her; he could compare her revelations with others he had read in his studies. An intelligent, knowledgeable listener! He was exactly what Catherine had hungered for. As soon as she could, she began to describe to him her visions of heaven and her conversations with her heavenly Bridegroom. She talked to him about God and man, about sin and grace; hour after hour she shared her insights and revelations.

Raymond felt buried in the avalanche of words. He did not trust the endless outpouring of visions and revelations and spiritual favors that she described. There were too many words, too many unprovable spiritual ideas. "I would rather stick to the five senses," he thought one night after he had spent several hours listening to the young visionary. The next morning he was called to her bedside where she lay, too ill to rise, but not too ill to continue her conversation of the night before. He was irritated by her talk, reluctant to believe any of it.

He looked down at her face as she lay there, and saw, not Catherine's face, but the face of Christ. "Who is this who is looking at me?" he cried.

"It is He who is," Catherine answered. Raymond knew then that Catherine was not a hoax, but truly a disciple of Jesus. He subsequently became one of Catherine's staunchest supporters and defenders.[4]

He continued to be overpowered by her words, however. In his *Legend* he says that she had a greater appetite than he for talk about God. She would be energized by such conversations, but he would fall asleep. She might go on for hours without noticing, and then when she saw that he was sleeping, she would be furious. "Have I been talking to the wall or to you?" she would demand. "Have you no interest in the knowledge of God? For the sake of a little sleep would you neglect the state of your soul?"

Raymond was a man of moderation. Catherine was never moderate, not in her penances, not in her enthusiasm, certainly not in her love for Christ. This contrast in their personalities served them well.

With Raymond at her side as her loyal listener and adviser, Catherine's life began to change. She was no longer Siena's private holy woman — she belonged to all of Tuscany now. She continued to work with the poor and the sick and to pray for the conversion of sinners. Her work continued to bring about miraculous cures and dramatic changes of heart. People from all the surrounding area knew about Catherine and wanted to see her.

Wherever she went, crowds appeared. People recognized her as a holy woman, one to whom God had given special powers. No one ever saw her eat. She fell into ecstatic trances and even levitated. These were all considered mysterious and undeniable signs of holiness. Besides all this, she worked miracles.

"Miracles." The people hungered for miracles. If only they could see a miracle, everything would be easier. If only God would suspend His natural laws, even for a moment, they would know for certain that He was real. There is no logic to this position, yet it has persisted over the centuries.

Jesus became impatient with those who hungered for miracles. He told the scribes and Pharisees when they asked Him to work some signs for them: "An evil and unfaithful age is eager for a sign!" (Matthew 12:39). Saint Paul, too, became exasperated with miracle seekers. He declared: "Yes, Jews demand 'signs' and Greeks look for 'wisdom,' but we preach Christ crucified — a stumbling block to Jews, and an absurdity to Gentiles; but to those who are called, Jews and Greeks alike, Christ the power of God and the wisdom of God" (1 Corinthians 1:22-24).

In Jesus' time, in Paul's, and in all ages since, miracles have drawn crowds. People come out to see the miracle worker, and stay to hear God's message. That continued to happen in Catherine's day. She was asked to visit and teach all over Tuscany and Lombardy; and wherever she went, the crowds were so vast and her preaching so effective that three priests had to travel with her to hear the confessions of the faithful and the converts. By papal decree the three were granted special authority to absolve sins that ordinarily required absolution by a bishop.

She spent six months preaching in Pisa and the surrounding area. Raymond of Capua described what it was like to be on that mission. The lines of people waiting to go to confession would stretch around churches and across fields. The priests would start hearing confessions at dawn and sometimes work till the evening curfew, without ever stopping to eat. They would be exhausted by the press of people, discouraged by the endless lines, but not Catherine. The sight of so many people repenting and turning to Jesus gave her fresh energy. She would pray more and more fervently as the day wore on, thanking her Savior and Lord for the greatness of His mercy, exultant and rejoicing over each repentant sinner.

Catherine did not seek crowds and she did not promote herself as a miracle worker. Her concern always was for the salvation of souls. The miracles she prayed for most often were the conversion of sinners and the reconciliation of enemies. She prayed that people would have the grace to understand the will of God and cooperate with it. She gave her attention to the invisible world of the spirit, not the world of the flesh. Even so, her fame continued to grow. She prayed, for instance, for the conversion of a young nobleman named Niccolo di Toldo.

He had been out drinking one night and, under the influence of wine, he criticized the ruling clique in Siena. He meant his remark to be a joke, but it was overheard by the wrong people. Poor Niccolo, barely out of his teens, was jailed and sentenced to death. His life was going to end before it had even begun, and all for a few words spoken in jest, words that meant nothing.

He was terrified. He was angry and depressed, too; but more than anything else he was scared. Tommaso Caffarini said Niccolo paced up and down in his cell like a madman, unwilling to go to confession or even talk to a priest, unwilling to deal with a God who would allow such a meaningless death. His distraught family begged Catherine to visit him.

She went, and Niccolo was "be-Catherined." She gave him such comfort that he agreed to go to confession and prepare himself for death, on the condition that she would be with him at his execution. He was young and concerned with his honor. He did not want to disgrace himself in public. If Catherine was with him, he was sure he could be brave.

Catherine spent hours with him, preparing him for what was to come. "You will be going to your marriage feast!" she told him and he believed her. On the day he was to be beheaded they went to Mass together and he received Holy Communion for the first time in his life. After Mass they had to be parted for a few minutes while they made their separate ways to the execution site.

"Be of good courage, my sweet brother," Catherine called to him, "for soon shall we enter into the everlasting marriage feast: you shall go there bathed in the sweet blood of the Son of God, with the sweet name of Jesus, which must never pass from your memory. And I await you at the place of execution."

Niccolo was filled with joy and replied, "How can it be that such abundant grace is granted to me, that the sweetness of my soul awaits me at the holy place of execution?"

When he arrived at the block, Catherine was already there, waiting and praying for him. He asked for her blessing, and she gave it gladly, making the Sign of the Cross over him as he knelt. With great tenderness she placed his head on the block and whispered, "Up to the marriage, my dear brother; soon shall you be in life everlasting." The executioner readied his blade. Niccolo looked at Catherine. "Jesus and Catherine," he whispered, "Jesus and Catherine."

The blade fell, separating head from shoulders. Niccolo's head rolled into Catherine's lap and she hugged it joyfully, praising God's mercy. Still clutching the young man's head, she prayed and saw Jesus receive Niccolo's spilled blood, and receive his soul, too, placing it in the "open treasure-house of his side." She knew, then, that her prayers had been answered and that Niccolo was at the wedding feast at last. Her soul rested in peace, smelling the fragrance of the blood which seemed to her "so sweet that I could not bear to wash from off my habit the blood that had sprinkled it."[5]

Many prominent citizens of Siena were present at Niccolo's execution and saw how bravely he walked to his death because of Catherine. More than ever before, wealthy and influential families sought her help.

The Maconi family sought her help. They had a son, Stephen, who was the pride of their lives — handsome, witty, charming, everything a young man should be. But he was caught up in a feud with the sons of the Rinaldi and Tolomei clans. All of the young men were traveling about armed, ready to spill their enemies' blood, or their own. Stephen's mother was sure he would be killed if Catherine did not intervene. The distraught mother pleaded with her son to talk to the holy woman. At last he agreed to go.

"She received me," Stephen wrote later, "not with the timidity of a young girl, but like a sister who was welcoming a brother returned from a distant journey. Full of astonishment, I listened to the words she addressed to me, exhorting me to confess and lead a Christian life. I said to myself, 'The finger of God is here.' "

Catherine, who was known and loved by the Tolomei family because of a miracle she had worked in the life of one of their relatives, arranged for a meeting of the three families to work out a plan for peace. The Maconi family came at the appointed time as promised, but the other two did not appear. "Very well," said Catherine, "if they won't listen to me, they will have to listen to God." She retired to a nearby church, prostrated herself before the main altar, and was soon rapt in ecstatic prayer.

Within minutes, the elders of the Tolomei and Rinaldi families walked into the church and saw her, lifted from the ground in prayer, her face surrounded with light. They were so impressed with her holiness that they immediately put the whole feud into her hands and agreed on any terms of peace she proposed.

The others left, satisfied because peace was arranged; but Stephen stayed on with Catherine, becoming one of her secretaries and, except for Raymond, her closest friend. "I left my father, my mother, my brothers and sisters, and all my kindred with joy," he wrote, "so happy was I to remain in Catherine's presence, and to be admitted to her holy friendship."[6]

These were happy years in Catherine's life, these years when Father Raymond of Capua was with her. Though her health had begun to fail, she still had energy enough to travel, preach, and pray for conversions. She had loyal friends to visit in all the major cities of the region, and, of course, her special circle of friends in Siena. Spiritually, too, she continued to grow and receive extraordinary graces from God.

From early childhood Catherine had been called by Jesus to unite herself with Him in more and more intimate ways. As He prepared her for each new stage in their union, He gave her a sign to help her understand the new life to which He was calling her. First came the vision, when she was just six years old, in which Jesus looked at her with love and invited her to follow Him. Later, when she was a teenager, living a life of fasting and isolation, she experienced a spiritual espousal to Jesus and received the ring that only she could see. Still later she received the crown of thorns, as she freely rejected a life of comfort and chose a life of suffering for His sake. Then there was an incident in which Jesus took away her heart and replaced it with His own. During this exchange Catherine told her confessor that she was without a heart for several days after Jesus took away her own "stony" heart, until He replaced it with His own tender heart with which to love His people.

The next and most mysterious of these experiences that transformed Catherine into the image of Christ happened during her triumphant mission to Pisa. Raymond, her confessor, was present. He had just said Mass for Catherine and her companions. She was rapt in prayer. "The soul that sighed after its Creator separated as much as it could from the body," Raymond said. Her companions watched her and waited for her to return to her senses, anxious to hear what happened. Often she returned with special messages and instructions for them. On this day, however, as they watched they saw her body, which had been lying prostrate, rise up and kneel, her face glowing as if a fire burned inside it. Then her body shuddered and collapsed upon the floor. A few minutes later Catherine awoke and went immediately to Raymond.

"Father, I must tell you that, by His mercy, I now bear the stigmata of the Lord Jesus in my body," she said. "I saw our Lord fastened to the cross, coming down upon me in a blaze of light. With that, as my spirit leaped to meet its Creator, this poor body was pulled upright. Then I saw, springing from the marks on His most sacred wounds, five blood-red rays coming down upon me, directed towards my hands and feet and heart. Realizing the meaning of this mystery, I promptly cried out: 'Ah, Lord, my God, I implore You not to let the marks show outwardly on my body.' Whilst these words were still upon my lips, before the rays had reached me, their blood-red color changed to radiant brightness, and it was in the form of clearest light that they fell upon the five parts of my body — hands, feet and heart."

Raymond questioned her concerning the fifth wound, assuming that it was in her side, but she insisted that it was in her heart.

The stigmata were a source of great pain to Catherine and produced in her an overwhelming sensation of physical weakness. She was no stranger to pain, but the pain that came with the wounds of Christ was so great that she soon lost consciousness and for a week she drifted in and out of a coma. She asked her followers to pray for her, convinced that she was dying, as Jesus had, feeling the torture of the nails. Raymond thought that she was dying, too, and sent word to her closest friends and family to come and pray for her.

The next Sunday brought her some relief, however, and she reported to Raymond, "The Lord has heard your prayers, and it is now my soul which is afflicted with suffering; but as for my body, those wounds no longer cause it pain, but rather lend it force and vigor. I can feel strength flowing into me from those wounds which at first only added to my sufferings."[7]

Some of Catherine's followers reported that after her death the stigmata became visible. Other observers who were present at her death make no mention of the phenomenon. Mother Theodosia Drane, writing about the stigma in Catherine's hand, which is preserved as a sacred relic in the convent of Saints Domenico and Sisto in Rome, says, "If by a stigma we are to understand an open wound or scar, this assertion is certainly not correct. Nevertheless, the precious relic does exhibit in the center of the palm an appearance as though all the substance of the hand under the skin had in that part been pierced, or removed; so that when a lighted candle is placed behind it, a spot of light becomes distinctly visible."[8]

6

A Day with Catherine and Her Friends

Catherine came home from Pisa bearing the invisible stigmata and the pain and weakness that accompanied them. Getting out of bed was hard for her practically every morning now. She still did not sleep more than an hour most nights, but she did rest in the early morning hours. After her rest, her body often felt weak. Later in the day she might find more energy, but never in the morning. Only the strength of her loyal friends among the Mantellate and the prospect of receiving the Eucharist could get her out of bed most mornings.

Receiving the Eucharist was the central event in Catherine's day. For many years it was her only food. It fed her physically and spiritually, and she hungered for it in both her body and her soul. When priests refused to give her the Holy Sacrament, as they often did before Raymond came to Siena, it caused her physical and spiritual anguish.

The priests at the cathedral of San Domenico did not welcome Catherine's presence at Mass, even after the finding of the general chapter in Florence. Neither they, nor her superiors in the Mantellate, approved of daily reception of the Eucharist and saw no need to encourage Catherine in this matter.

Their policy was that she could receive from her confessor and no one else. If her confessor was out of town or ill, Catherine would just have to wait until he could accommodate her.

At such times she said she would find comfort just looking at a priest. Her sight, which was always sensitive to spiritual realities, saw not only the sins that rotted souls but also the holy effects of the Eucharist on those who touch it and speak the words of consecration and consume it regularly. If she could not receive the food she craved, she could at least see the hands that held the food.

Raymond understood her need. She had only to say to him, "Father, I hunger," and he would arrange to say Mass if he could.

Later on, after she became known to Gregory XI (the last of the Avignon popes), and her special spiritual needs were understood, she received a papal bull giving her permission to receive Communion daily, and even to have an altar set up in her room so a priest could say Mass there if she was unable to get to a church. Until she received the bull, Raymond did his best to schedule Mass at a time when she could be there.

Extraordinary things happened to Catherine at Mass. She often reported that she saw visions, especially during the consecration. She might see Jesus in the priest's robes, repeating the words of the Last Supper; or when the priest raised the Sacred Host for all to adore, she might see the Infant Jesus in his hands. These visions kept the reality of the Blessed Sacrament fresh and vivid to her.

One day a priest decided to put her to a test, and gave her an unconsecrated host, pretending that it was Holy Communion. Catherine was not fooled in the least and had sharp words for a priest who would do such a thing to a person who hungered for Christ's body and blood.

The priests who said Mass for her regularly had their share of extraordinary experiences in her presence. Several reported that they felt the Blessed Sacrament move toward Catherine without their help. Some said the Host nodded toward her, or pulled their hands toward her. Raymond of Capua even reported that one day a piece of the Blessed Sacrament actually traveled across the church to her. Many of the priests, including Raymond, reported that Catherine's appearance changed after she received Communion. At times they could not recognize her face, it was so transformed; at times they believed they saw a glorified Catherine surrounded by light.

After receiving the Eucharist, Catherine was often lifted in ecstasy. If she was still in church her friends would stay with her, Alessia Saracini, her sister-in-law Lisa, and a Mantellata named Cecca (not to be confused with the leper Cecca in Chapter 3). When Catherine was able to walk again, they would all go back to her room, or to Alessia's house. Ecstasies exhausted Catherine. This had always been true: even when she was a child, praying in the cave like a hermit, her experience left her so weak she had trouble walking home. Now in her late twenties, her body permanently weakened by years of fasting and self-mortification, she was slow recovering her strength after the intense experience of this kind of prayer. She would need a long period of rest in bed, followed by quiet activities with her Mantellate friends: praying, talking, cooking.

She no longer had the boundless energy she used to have, when she scrubbed and cooked all day, and then washed all the family laundry at night. When a real need arose, she could still find the energy to do what had to be done. But most days she found quiet ways indoors to serve the Lord with her sisters of the Mantellate.

We know very little about the everyday life of Catherine and her loyal female friends. The people who wrote firsthand accounts of her life were all men, and they did not take part in the daytime routine or the rituals of female friendship. They mention the Mantellate only occasionally. Yet even their brief references give some idea of how the women lived. For instance, they tell us that whenever Catherine traveled, the women went with her to take care of her bodily needs. When they list the women, they always mention Alessia, Lisa, and Cecca; sometimes they name others, too, but always these three. They were true friends who stuck by Catherine in good times and bad till the day of her death.

Raymond said of Alessia that her need to be with Catherine was so great that she arranged her whole life so she would always be ready to serve her holy friend. She delegated the management of her property to others so she could always be free. Her life, her house, everything she owned, was at Catherine's disposal.

The women cooked together. That was one way they spent their time and built their friendship. When Catherine first rejoined her family, she did a lot of cooking for them, and Lisa helped her. We get glimpses of how easily they worked together from Raymond when he tells about miracles that occurred. One day, for instance, Catherine fell into a trance while turning the meat on a spit. Lisa came into the kitchen to help her serve the meal, saw that she was rapt in prayer, and took the spit out of her hand, leaving her to pray. When Lisa returned to the kitchen, she found that Catherine had fallen into the fire. She pulled her out and, according to Raymond, was astonished to find that though she had been lying on red-hot coals, she was not even burned.

As the years went by, Catherine continued to cook with her friends, and miracles continued to prompt men to write about them. The year after the plague, famine hit the region. The harvest had been poor in the plague year, because so few men were left to tend the fields. The next season brought drought, followed by famine. The price of grain was so high that only the rich could afford bread. Many poor families were starving, so Catherine and Alessia began baking bread for the hungry. Day after day they worked side by side stretching the bit of flour Alessia could find to make as many loaves as possible.

Many stories are told about the bread they baked. Some said that although Alessia's flour was a year old and moldy, the bread Catherine made from it was sweet and wholesome. Others said that Catherine could make many more loaves from the same measure of flour than her friends could. Still others reported that although Alessia had only a little flour left at the beginning of the famine, she never ran out as long as they made bread for the poor.

Some of Catherine's women friends could write, and though they did not write biographical accounts, they did write letters to her and she to them. They tend to be practical, sometimes even homey, letters. When Catherine wrote to men, she defined the problems of the world, or at least of nations, and proposed solutions to them. When she wrote to women, she wrote about how to handle grief, and how to raise children, how to fast and not to fast. In letters to a few very close friends she wrote about the dangers and difficulties of an intense spiritual life; she even revealed her own weaknesses and failures in her spiritual struggle.

Many women did not get along well with Catherine. One good example, as we have already seen, was her mother. Lapa loved her daughter fiercely, but disagreed with almost everything Catherine did and the way she wanted to do it. Some of the older women in the Mantellate distrusted Catherine because she did not act the way other women did: she traveled around too much, she made too much noise in church, she drew too much attention to herself. Perhaps some of these women were jealous of Catherine, or perhaps they were afraid of her because she was so different. Stories and rumors about Catherine circulated among the women of Siena, and many of them were neither true nor complimentary.

The women who were loyal to Catherine were enraged by these rumors and driven by them to be even more protective of their "beloved Mama." The picture that emerges of Catherine and her daily companions is a picture of close friends who spent a lot of time together, praying and doing female chores: cooking, sewing, and teaching children.

Catherine's relationships with men were different. With them she was lofty, theological, authoritarian. Catherine treated women as her peers, but with men she was always in charge. She entered their world and understood it, perhaps better than they did. She told them, without hesitation, what they should do, and they accepted her advice gratefully. Many men were suspicious of Catherine before they met her, but once they knew her they were "be-Catherined." They became her supporters and even her disciples.

Most evenings these men visited Catherine and her Mantellate friends. They all prayed together. Often Catherine taught them, sharing her newest insights and revelations. She may have lacked energy in the mornings, but not in the evenings when there were people who liked to hear her talk about God. She listened to them, too, as they told her their problems, and she gave them spiritual direction.

These evenings that Catherine spent with her followers were exciting times for all of them. They learned so much from her, and they grew so much closer to God. In that atmosphere, so full of God's love, they all learned to love one another. Few people can boast of so many friends or such deep love as Catherine shared with her friends. The young girl who emerged from the silence of her cell ten years earlier, unsure of how to talk to people or form friendships, had learned a lot. Yet she never found it easy to be a friend; she never found it easy to be with people. She told Raymond that she prayed daily for the gift of love because she felt so inadequate in friendship. Her favorite companion was Jesus. Leaving Him, leaving prayer to be with people, was like leaving home to be in exile. She did it because He told her to, not because it was what she wanted.

In *The Dialogue*, she wrote, "This is how it is with very dear friends. Their loving affection makes them two bodies with one soul, because love transforms one into what one loves. And if these souls are made one soul, nothing can be kept hidden from them.''[1] That was the kind of love Catherine had for Jesus, a love that transformed her into Him. Her whole life was lived in imitation of Christ. There is no evidence that she ever had this kind of love for her friends on earth, no evidence that she ever tried to become like Raymond of Capua, or Stephen Maconi, or Alessia Saracini. But the reverse may have been true: many of her followers wanted to grow like her, as she wanted to grow like Christ.

Some of her friends tried to describe what it was like to be in her presence. One said that people always trembled when they beheld her because the power of the Spirit was so strong in her. Another described her as glowing from within, as if she were on fire. "She is here on the earth, but she lives her life in heaven," said Francesco Malavolti, "and it makes a miserable creature like me giddy merely to think of it!" Neri de' Pagliaresi agreed, adding, "That is why she can be what she is to us, our venerable, joyous and sweetest Mamma."[2]

Being with Catherine was, above all, a spiritual experience. Those who were with her became aware of the presence of God within them, knowing them, loving them, and helping them on the road to salvation. It was a comfort to experience God in this way; it was a comfort to be with Catherine.

It was not always easy, of course. Pope Gregory XI would find, when he was with Catherine, that God would give him faith and courage, which were very comforting; He also gave the pope the sure knowledge that he had to act. God was with him, but God expected something from him.

Often those who met Catherine found their own sin revealed to them with unmistakable clarity. This was what happened to Fra Lazzarino of Pisa, the wise Franciscan who let the revelation transform his life.

Catherine, as has been pointed out, was a spiritual director to the men who surrounded her. She had gifts that made her an excellent director. She could smell sin. She and her disciples mention this gift often, especially in stories about how she knew when someone needed to go to confession. She could see souls; she saw their beauty and the effect of sin on them. She could see, almost like a picture, the spiritual condition of those she prayed for. Sometimes she could see the spiritual condition of persons who weren't even in the same room, or even in the same country.

She believed God had entrusted her friends to her to ensure their salvation, and she did not want to lose any of them. She prayed for each of them daily, checking on the health of their souls.

Of all the men who called Catherine their friend, two stand out because of the depth of their friendship with her. Two could give Catherine something she needed. The first of these men was Raymond of Capua. The friendship between Catherine and Raymond, which began in the heady days after her triumph at the Dominican general chapter and continued during the time of the Black Death, matured and deepened as time went by. Raymond was her confessor for only six years, and during those years he was often away on missions for the pope. Yet he had a tremendous influence on her life.

In a letter she wrote to him in 1377 she gave him as high a compliment as a Christian could receive. "Sweetest father," she wrote, "your soul has made itself food for me."[3] Catherine needed Raymond as she needed no other human being. She needed his attention, his intelligence, and perhaps even his approval.

The other man who gave Catherine something beyond adoring approval was that handsome young charmer, Stephen Maconi. He was a man women liked. Catherine enjoyed his company and so did his mother. Some of Catherine's most interesting letters were written to Stephen's mother, explaining why she was so sure that God wanted Stephen to be with Catherine and not at home taking care of his widowed mother.

Stephen enjoyed a special relationship with Catherine.

He said that he was the "Benjamin" of the group, the youngest and best-loved son. "She loved me with the tenderness of a mother, far more than I deserved, so as to inspire some of her children with a kind of envy," he said.

Stephen stayed with her during the long nights while the others slept, writing down her letters as she dictated them, listening to her late-night thoughts. "Never did an idle word fall from her mouth," he reported. "Our most frivolous conversations she knew how to turn to our spiritual profit. If anyone spoke in her presence of worldly things, she took refuge in contemplation, and then her body would become wholly insensible. Her whole life was a miracle, but there was one circumstance about it truly admirable. Nothing that she did, said, or heard, hindered her soul from being intimately united to God, and plunged as it were into the Divinity."[4]

Stephen did not feel that he was plunged into the Divinity. He was attracted by the spiritual world, but equally attracted by the world of wealth and frivolity that he knew before he met Catherine. For most of his life he felt torn between these two worlds. He found peace only in Catherine's presence, where the power of the Spirit within her made the attractions of this world seem as nothing to him. When he had to be separated from her, he was thrown into spiritual agony.

Catherine understood this conflict within Stephen, perhaps better than he did. She believed that Christ's will for him, as it had been for the rich young man of the Gospel, was to sell all he possessed, give up everything, and follow Him. She tried to prepare him to accept this radical message as she directed his spiritual growth over the years.

Stephen was not the only young man who stayed up with Catherine. The poet Neri de' Pagliaresi and his friend Francesco Malavolti, as well as several other wealthy and educated young men, loved to be with her at night, listening to her private thoughts, writing her letters as she dictated them. These letters soon drew her into a whole new kind of service to

God and the Church, as she became involved in the politics of the Church and the papacy.

At first most of the letters she dictated were personal: to her new friends in Florence and Pisa and other parts of Tuscany, to people who sought spiritual counseling. She wrote to one of her nieces on the occasion of her First Holy Communion. She wrote to her oldest brother telling him to pay more attention to his mother. She answered the letter of a priest who thought it was the devil who gave her the power to fast so long.

Soon she was dictating other kinds of letters: letters to city officials telling them what to do about specific problems, letters to prominent priests and bishops with advice on how to run their affairs. When Gregory XI was elected pope and he called for a new crusade, she wrote praising his idea and offering support. She wrote to kings and queens, heads of state, military leaders and common brigands, urging them to support the pope's new venture.

This series of letters about launching a crusade is of special interest because through this correspondence Catherine and Gregory XI started a friendship that would influence the course of the Church for generations, even centuries, to come.

The first of the letters between Catherine and Gregory XI have been lost. But letters she wrote to other people about the crusade have survived, showing her style and thoughts about the undertaking.

She wrote to the king of France, telling him that it was God's will that he make peace with England so that both countries could send their armies on the crusade. "I tell you on behalf of Christ crucified," she wrote, "that you must delay no longer to make this peace. Make peace, and direct all your warfare to the infidels. Help to encourage and uplift the standard of the most holy Cross which God shall demand from you and others at the point of death. . . . Sleep no more, for love of Christ crucified, and for your own profit, during the little time that remains to us: for time is short, and you are to die, and know not when."[5]

It is typical of Catherine's style when writing to men in authority that she would tell them what God wanted them to do, and in this connection would often use the phrase "on behalf of Christ crucified." She also often reminded them, as she did here, that life is short, and when it is over, Christ will demand an accounting of our stewardship.

She wrote to an Englishman named John Hawkwood, the leader of a band of mercenary soldiers who committed dreadful atrocities in Tuscany during the famine. "It is high time now that you thought a little of yourself and considered how great are the sufferings you have borne so long in serving the devil. My soul desires that you now change your manner of life and with all your followers enter the service of Christ crucified, so that henceforth you may be a company of Christ, going to war against the infidel dogs who have possession of our holy places — there where the sweet Truth Himself suffered death for us. I entreat you then, in Christ Jesus, that since you take so much delight in warfare and fighting, not to fight any longer against Christian men, but rather against unbelievers. . . ."[6]

Catherine was stepping boldly into the affairs of men, delivering God's message to men in high places. She seemed never to doubt the truth of her message, even when she called human beings "infidel dogs." Her letters were blunt, vivid, and numerous.

She spent hours dictating to her secretaries. She prayed, dictated, and prayed again. Some nights she kept five men busy as she dictated part of one letter to one secretary, then part of another letter to the next, and so on, around the room. Sometimes she dictated while she was in ecstasy. Much of *The Dialogue* was written this way. Someone was always on hand to take down anything she said aloud while she was praying: letters, prayers, poems, advice for friends, passages for *The*

Book, as she called her great work that we know as *The Dialogue*.

As dawn broke, Catherine would collapse on her bed of boards, exhausted from her long night's work. She might sleep a little; more likely she would rest and prepare herself to receive Holy Communion once again, and start a new day of prayer and service to the Lord.

7

Catherine Fights Corruption in the Church

Brother Gabriel of Volterra, master of sacred theology and master-provincial of the Order of Friars Minor, lay in his canopied bed and relaxed for a few minutes before rising. He looked forward to the meal he would share later in the day with Father John Tantucci, prior of the ancient monastery of Lecceto of the Order of Augustinian Hermits, also a master of sacred theology. Brother Gabriel stretched, relishing the feel of the smooth silk sheets. He glanced about his room and liked what he saw. He had designed his quarters himself, instructing friars where to tear down old walls to make one new room out of three old cells. The furnishings, too, reflected Brother Gabriel's impeccable taste and attention to detail. Each painting, each piece of sculpture, each magnificently bound book was appropriately displayed. It was a room worthy of one of the Church's great scholars and teachers.

Later that day when the two friends dined, they talked about the ignorant young woman from nearby Siena who had been drawing so much attention to herself by performing supposed miracles.

"You would think the Dominicans would stop her," Brother Gabriel said.

"It is a scandal!" Brother Gabriel went on. "She presumes to teach others. And has the little woman ever studied theology? Of course not. Or Sacred Scripture? Can she even read? Who would have taught her? That woman could lead hundreds astray. Even thousands."

"Perhaps the Dominicans don't know how to stop her," Father Tantucci responded, "or perhaps they don't see the danger. But we see the danger, don't we, my friend? And I am sure that we could find a way to stop her. Would you like to try? For the good of Holy Church of course?"

The concerns of the two learned men were well founded. These were difficult days for the Church. Most of the faithful were illiterate and unschooled in the teachings of the Church. Parish priests were often only slightly better educated; they were taught enough Latin to say Mass and administer the sacraments, but they were not scholars or theologians. In the midst of such ignorance, heresies, once taught, could spread throughout a province. Correcting heresies was hard to do and had led the Church to take drastic, sometimes even brutal, actions. It was better if heresies did not start.

The two scholars decided to visit Catherine that evening and expose her ignorance. Their aim was not to listen to her, only to shame her in front of her followers, and thus end her teaching days forever.

During the three-mile walk to Siena they worked out their questions. They did not want to miss a chance to reveal her ignorance.

Catherine, in the meantime, was in her little room, talking as usual with her friends about God. Francesco Malavolti later wrote about what happened that evening. Catherine stopped talking suddenly and began to pray with great fervor, her face glowing with love.

After a time she turned her attention again to her friends. She smiled gently. "Soon," she said, "you will see two great fish caught in a net." Her followers didn't understand what she meant and they didn't have time to ask because at that moment a servant announced that Brother Gabriel of Volterra and Father John Tantucci were at the door asking permission to see Catherine.

She greeted them and found places for them on her bench. She herself sat at their feet, and her friends stood about.

The learned men were ready. First Brother Gabriel, and then Father John fired questions at her. Catherine leaned toward them, listening intently to the scholars.

When they finished, and it was time for her to respond, she lashed out at them, "How can you begin to understand anything that pertains to the kingdom of God? You who live only for the world, and seek to be honored by men. . . . Your great learning is no help to you or to others. It only harms you because you seek the shell and not the core!" Looking directly at Brother Gabriel she demanded, "How can you, a son of Saint Francis, dare to live the way you do? For the sake of Jesus Christ crucified do not live this way any longer!"[1]

Brother Gabriel of Volterra was silent for a moment. Then he fell on his knees before her. He took the keys from his belt and handed them to Catherine saying, "Is there anyone here who would go to my room and strip it of everything I own? I want to have nothing but the clothes on my back and my breviary. Everything else should be used for the poor. Never again will I live as I have done. I will follow my father Francis until the end of my days."

The Franciscan scholar lived a reformed life as he had promised. Soon afterward he left the friary where he was master-provincial and went to Florence to spend the rest of his days waiting on his fellow friars, cooking and serving their meals.

Father John Tantucci, too, repented and sold all that he owned, though he did not own as much as his friend. He stayed with Catherine and became one of her most faithful disciples, traveling with her to Avignon and to Rome, and serving as one of the priests who heard confessions when she went abroad to preach.

Father John and Brother Gabriel were not the only clergymen living in luxury and ignoring their true callings. Pride and self-indulgence were a pestilence that ravaged the Church in the fourteenth century. In a letter to Pope Gregory XI, Catherine wrote that the first great task God expected of him as pope was to reform the Church. "Uproot in the garden of Holy Church," she said in her letter, "the malodorous flowers, full of impurity and avarice, swollen with pride: that is, the bad priests and rulers who poison and rot that garden. Throw them away that they may have no rule! Insist that they study to rule themselves in holy and good lives. Plant in this garden fragrant flowers, priests and rulers who are true servants of Jesus Christ. Alas, what confusion is this, to see those who ought to be a mirror of voluntary poverty, meek as lambs, distributing the possessions of Holy Church to the poor; and they appear in such luxury and state and pomp and worldly vanity."[2]

Gregory XI himself lived in "pomp and worldly vanity." He had not designed his sumptuous living arrangement himself, as Gabriel of Volterra had. But the papal court in Avignon over which he presided was hardly a "mirror of voluntary poverty" where the possessions of the Church were distributed to the poor. On the contrary it was a place where popes and their advisers lived in unbelievable wealth and luxury and wielded power for their own benefit and that of their families and friends.

The popes had power to wield in the fourteenth century. The Church owned vast properties and extensive lands. Popes could raise armies and fight wars. They could issue an interdict that would bring economic disaster to a country. And they could excommunicate anyone who did not like their policies.

They held this power in a world that was politically unstable. Other states had about the same amount of power and wealth, and all were vying to see who would prove strongest, who could dominate the others. The popes took part in this struggle, like any other head of state. Wars were frequent; atrocities and abuse of power were commonplace, even in the Papal States.

But when the papal court was moved from Rome to Avignon in 1309, new ways for popes to abuse power were discovered. The move took place during the papacy of Clement V. Civil war and revolution made Rome a dangerous place to live. A pope was even kidnapped and beaten during an uprising in Rome. Clement V wanted to find a safer place for his court. The king of France invited him to use the royal palaces in the beautiful city of Avignon, where they could be safe and secure, living under the protection of the French army. Clement accepted the invitation. He and his next six successors — all Frenchmen, living in Avignon — built a series of sumptuous palaces and courtyards and fortifications, the most splendid court in all Europe, some called it.

Others called it Babylon. "A fountain of affliction, a house of wrath, a school of error, a temple of heresy," were a few of the names the Italian poet Petrarch used for the papal court in Avignon. He did not object to beautiful buildings, but to the rampant evil that thrived within them: drunkenness, debauchery, promiscuity. Another famous Italian poet, Dante, railed against the sin of Avignon, too; so did Saint Bridget (or Birgitta) of Sweden.

When Gregory XI became pope, the court was already established as a seat of luxury and sin. The sisters and nieces and mistresses of the cardinals were as prominent in Avignon as their counterparts were in any court in Europe. In opulent salons, courtiers and courtesans sipped coffee from tiny cups and decided which witty and fashionable bishop should be granted which lucrative post.

Pope Gregory XI was not an evil man, nor was he addicted to luxuries. But he was surrounded by friends and relatives who were sure that a life of luxury and the wielding of power were their birthright. For nearly a century the positions of power and wealth in the Church had been held by a few French families. That was the only Church they knew or imagined. They saw the Church as an institution of worldly power. They understood that power and were expert at using it. The purpose of that power, as they saw it, was to make the Church strong and, in turn, to make them strong. It never occurred to them that power should be used to help and protect the poor.

This attitude spread from Avignon to every corner of the Church, dominating the thinking of bishops, priests, and leaders of religious orders and convents.

Catherine's view of the Church was radically different. She was aware of the worldly, institutional dimension of the Church; but she was even more aware of its spiritual nature, the channel through which God's grace flows to men. She believed that the greatest strength of the Church was spiritual, not material.

She saw the Church as it was meant to be, the spotless bride of Christ, living in loving obedience to the will of the Savior and Lord. She saw it in its spiritual reality, the Mystical Body of Christ, continuing His work on earth: loving, teaching, healing, serving His people.

"The Church is no other than Christ Himself, and it is she who gives us the Sacraments, and the Sacraments give us life,"[3] she wrote. Her great desire was to restore the Church to right order, where, on earth, as in heaven, all people might see Jesus as their King, reaching out to them with love.

Catherine has often been called a "reformer" of the Church. But she never wanted to change the form of the Church; she never tried to reorganize it in any way. She saw the organization as a divine creation, perfect as it was. What she wanted to change was the sinful lives of the members of the

Church, especially the clergy, "the ministers of the blood" as she often called them, who were not living in a manner worthy of their calling. She also wanted all the faithful — clergy and lay people alike — to obey those in authority, especially the pope, whom she called "sweet Christ on earth."

According to a major revelation she received on the night of April 1, 1376, Catherine believed that she had been chosen and empowered by Jesus to carry out this work of purification.

She described in a letter to Raymond of Capua, who was in Avignon at the time, what happened: "God revealed His mysteries to me and showed me His wonderful counsels in such a way that my soul no longer knew whether it was in the body, and I was filled with such abundant joy that my tongue has no power to express it."

Jesus revealed to her that the Church would undergo a time of persecution and purification, followed by a period of glory that would bring salvation to many. "I do as I did when I was here on earth and made a scourge of cords and drove out those who bought and sold in the temple. For I have made a scourge of men and with this scourge I drive out the unclean, covetous, miserly and proud peddlers who buy and sell the gifts of the Holy Spirit." Catherine understood that she was part of that scourge.

This revelation was followed by a vision. "I marveled," she wrote, "to see both Christians and infidels entering into the wound in the heart of Christ crucified, and I walked into the midst of them and entered into Christ sweet Jesus together with my father, Saint Dominic, and the Friend of my heart, John (her pet name for Raymond of Capua), and all my spiritual children. And then He laid the Cross upon my shoulder and placed the branch of olive in my hand, and said to me that I was to go out with it to all people. And He said to me: 'Go and tell them: behold I bring you tidings of great joy.' "[4]

Catherine believed she was sent by Jesus to go to the Church as a peacemaker; and as a scourge, to purify the

Church so that all people, Christian and infidel alike, could find salvation in Christ.

She wrote endless numbers of letters not only to the popes but also to bishops, cardinals, and priests, to kings and queens, to faithful and unfaithful members of the Church, telling them what they needed to do. She did not stop with writing letters. She journeyed great distances to push for reforms and to inspire the fainthearted with her own great moral courage. She made trips to Florence to negotiate a peace between that ambitious republic and the Papal States. She traveled throughout Tuscany urging the cities to remain loyal to the Holy Father.

Most of all she prayed and fasted and suffered, beseeching her heavenly Bridegroom through hundreds of long nightly vigils to have mercy on His Church and pour His grace upon its ministers so they could see their sins and change their lives.

Catherine was willing to suffer for the Church; she was also willing to fight. Her letters show her as God's scourge, determined to drive evil out of the Church.

She wrote, for instance, to a priest from Semignano who was plotting to kill a fellow priest as part of a blood feud. "Priest," she said, "live in peace with your Creator and make peace between His creatures. That is your duty and you ought to fulfill it. . . .

"Respect the exalted dignity of your state. . . . You represent the person of Christ when you consecrate His Sacrament. Therefore, you should love and reverence your dignity with great purity and with a peaceful heart, tearing out from your soul every hatred and desire of vengeance.

"You require a spotless purity in the chalice you use at the altar, and refuse to use one that is soiled; remember then, that God, the Sovereign Truth, demands a like purity in your soul. Woe is me! On all sides we behold the contrary. Those who should be the temples of God are the stables of swine: they carry the fire of hatred and vengeance, and an evil will in their souls. . . .

"I know not how you dare to celebrate. I declare to you that if you persevere in this hatred, and in your other vices, the wrath of God will burst over your head. Let there be an end of this, reform your life, and cast out from your heart all this misery, and above all, this deadly hate. I desire that you be both reconciled. What a disgrace to see two priests engaged in deadly hatred! It is a marvel to me that God does not command the earth to open and swallow you both up. . . . I will say no more; but reply to me, and tell me what is your will and intention. May you abide in the love of God."[5]

She wrote to Gerard du Puy, the man responsible for appointments of pastors and bishops in Tuscany, a key figure in Church reform. She was not subtle in her choice of words: "Our Lord holds in aversion three detestable vices above all others — they are impurity, avarice, and pride. And they all reign in the spouse of Christ — at least among her prelates, who seek after nothing but pleasures, honors, and riches. They see the demons of hell carrying off the souls confided to them, and they care nothing at all about it. . . ."

She went on to tell the pope's representative what he needed to do to solve the problem: "And when the time comes for choosing pastors and cardinals, let not flattery and money and simony have any part in their election; regard nothing but the good qualities of the persons proposed, and give no heed whether they are nobles or peasants. Virtue is the only thing which really makes a man noble, or pleasing to God."[6]

Catherine set high standards — for herself, for her friends, for priests and prelates, and especially for the Holy Father. Again and again she urged the popes, first Gregory XI and later Urban VI, to act like Christ: manly, forgiving, honest, loving.

Even if a pope did not act like "sweet Christ on earth," Catherine believed that the faithful should treat him with the respect and obedience they would show to Jesus Himself. "Even if he were an incarnate devil, we ought not to raise up our heads against him — but calmly lie down to rest on his bosom."[7]

She wrote to the Florentines, who were rebelling against Pope Gregory XI: "He who rebels against our Father, Christ on earth, is condemned to death, for that which we do to him, we do to Christ in heaven — we honor Christ if we honor the pope, we dishonor Christ if we dishonor the pope. . . . I tell you that God wills and has so commanded that even if the priests and the pastors of the Church and Christ on earth were incarnate devils, it is seemly that we are obedient and subject to them, not for their sake, but for the sake of God, out of obedience to Him, for He wills that we should act thus.

"Know that the son is never in the right against the father, even if the father is ever so evil and unjust, for so great is the good which he has received from the father, that is, life itself, that he can never repay him for it. And we have received the life of grace from the Church, which is so great a benefit, that we can never, by any kind of homage or gratitude, pay the debt we owe."[8]

But the fourteenth century was not an age when many people looked to their pope and Church with that sort of reverence. More often than not they saw the Church as an authority that had power, power that was used against its members. Tragically, this was often the case. For instance, when famine devastated Tuscany just after the plague, thousands of the faithful were starving. Papal lands, not far away, brought in abundant harvests that year, but no grain was sent by the French hierarchy to the starving Tuscans. It seemed to the Tuscans that the French hierarchy were always ready to take wealth away and never willing to give anything in return.

The people of Florence were particularly bitter against the French popes. Many of the reasons for the bitterness went back for generations, even centuries. By Catherine's day the tension was so great that small insults could flare into conflagrations. Florence decided to tax the clergy. Avignon was furious and sent a nuncio to protest. The Florentines flayed the man in the streets. The pope responded by putting the Republic of Florence under interdict, which had devastating effects. All churches were closed; all sacraments forbidden to Florentines. And on the economic level there was a worldwide boycott. Any Christian who did business with any Florentine was excommunicated. This meant economic disaster for Florence, a nation of merchants and traders, dependent on others for practically all their resources.

Catherine did everything she could to bring about peace. Both sides requested that she negotiate with them and for them, and she did, devoting months of her life, using all her considerable skills as a peacemaker. She urged the Florentines to be obedient and loyal sons; she urged the popes to be merciful and forgiving fathers. She failed utterly.

In sorrow Catherine wrote to her friends, "Now is the time to weep and mourn, for the bride of Christ is persecuted by her false and corrupt members. I therefore pray you, my daughters and sons, that you all pray . . . before the face of God for Holy Church, for she is sorely persecuted."[9]

The persecution, however, continued unabated. Florence broke openly with the pope and began to raise an army to oppose him. "Death to the princes of the Church," read one banner carried through the streets of Florence as its citizens stormed a castle where the French priests and bishops sought refuge. Hungering for revenge after generations of abuse, the Florentines built a catapult that they called "priest-killer," using it to hurl red-hot stones into the fortress.

Florence was not alone in its defiance of papal authority. Cities and towns throughout Tuscany were ready to defy Avignon. Catherine wrote letters and visited civil leaders urging them to remain loyal to the pope, but all her efforts were made in vain. The Tuscans felt too much resentment against the French clergy who had taxed them to pay for the pope's army, but refused them grain when they needed it.

"Fling off the yoke of the foreigner!" rang the cry. "The time has come to take up arms against the Church. Join the Florentines." More towns sided with Florence against Pope Gregory XI. When Perugia fell in behind all the others, Raymond of Capua brought the bad news to Catherine.

"You begin to weep too soon," she told him. "Save your tears for a better occasion. That which you see now is only milk and honey compared to what is to come."

"What could be worse?" Raymond wanted to know. "Will faith in Jesus Christ Himself be openly denied?"

"Today it is the laity who rebel against our sweet Christ on earth," Catherine replied, "but soon it will be the clergy who turn against him."

In later years Raymond remembered these words of Catherine's and understood them to be a prophecy concerning the great schism that was to break upon the Church within a few short years. "You will see them do it with your own eyes," she told him, "the moment he takes on to reform their evil conduct. They will raise a universal scandal throughout the holy Church of God, that will rend and ravish it like the pest of heresy itself."

Raymond asked her if there was to be another heresy. "No, not exactly a heresy," she replied, "but something like a heresy which will mean a cleavage in the Church and throughout Christendom. So now get ready to suffer, for you yourself will live to see these things."[10]

In spite of this ominous prediction, Catherine did all she could to strengthen the Church, to pull the warring parties back together, to bring the clergy to repentance. She did not succeed, but she never stopped trying.

Statue in Wood of Saint Catherine
By Neroccio Landi

*Saint Catherine
Praying for the Soul
of a Heretic*
By Sodoma

Saint Catherine Cures Matteo di Cenni of the Plague
By G. del Pacchia

Saint Catherine Receiving the Stigmata
By Sano di Pietro

Saint Catherine Chooses the Crown of Thorns
By A. Franchi

Saint Catherine's Head at San Domenico in Siena

Relics in Saint Catherine's House at Siena
Left: *Scent Bottle, Lantern, and Staff-head;* Center: *Veil and Hair Shirt;* Right: *Sack in Which Catherine's Head Was Brought from Rome*

Saint Catherine's House at Siena

The Church of San Domenico at Siena

Saint Catherine Persuades Pope Gregory XI to Return from Avignon to Rome
By Sebastiano Conca

The Swoon of Saint Catherine
By Sodoma

Saint Catherine
By Sodoma

Entrance to the Oratory in Saint Catherine's House at Siena

A Page from Saint Catherine's Missal

Saint Catherine and the Confraternity of the Misericordia
By Sano di Pietro

8

Catherine and Gregory

Before Catherine ever met Pope Gregory XI she had written to him many times, advising him about the affairs of the Church. He had written to her, too, and so had his advisers, seeking her counsel. In one letter she wrote about the defiant Florentines, urging the pope to forgive them and to welcome them back into the Church. "Babbo Mio," she wrote, "the wolf is carrying away your sheep, and there is no one found to help them. So I hasten to you, our father and our shepherd, begging you on behalf of Christ crucified to learn from Him, . . .

"Holiest sweet Babbo mine, I see no other way for us, and no other help in winning back your sheep, which have left the fold of Holy Church in rebellion, not obedient nor subject to you, their father. . . . I ask you, father, to show them mercy. Do not regard the ignorance and pride of your sons. . . .

"I tell you, sweet Christ on earth, on behalf of Christ in Heaven, that if you do thus, without any strife or tempest, they will all come, grieving for the wrong they have done, and will put their heads in your bosom. Then you will rejoice, and we shall rejoice, because by love you have restored the wandering sheep to the fold of Holy Church."[1]

In this letter and many others, Catherine addressed the

111

pope with affection and familiarity, and went on to tell him, without self-consciousness, what God wanted him to do. She was sure she knew God's will, and that the Holy Father needed to learn it from her. It might seem presumptuous on her part to think that God would reveal His will to her, and not to His anointed vicar on earth. But Catherine was neither the first holy woman, nor the last, to serve as a prophet who delivered God's message to a pope.

Her immediate predecessor in this role was Saint Bridget of Sweden, a mystic with strong opinions on the politics and policies of the Church, and the courage to speak them out boldly to the popes. Bridget was honored as a prophet by Gregory XI, but she was never considered a favorite of the court. Her messages were austere and harshly worded, terrible warnings about the doom that would descend on the Church unless the pope acted promptly.

By contrast, Catherine's letters on the same subjects, taking the same positions, seem full of the warmth and earthiness of sunny Italy, as she describes the Church as a garden that has been allowed to grow wild, or children who long for the comfort of their father's lap, or a wound that needs to be cauterized.

Gregory liked Catherine. He respected her ideas, as he had respected Saint Bridget's, in part because he agreed with them. But beyond that, he liked her. He enjoyed her company, as so many men did; he felt more of a man when he was with her.

They first met in 1376. Catherine went to Avignon at the request of Florence, which was on the brink of war with the pope. A group of moderates had come to power in Florence, and these moderates recognized Catherine as a holy person as well as a gifted peacemaker, someone the pope would respect, someone who would win sympathy for their cause. They were right.

Pope Gregory XI — whose respect and affection Catherine had won — put a beautiful house at her disposal, complete with furnishings and servants, everything she and her friends might need. At his insistence she stayed in Avignon for four months, conferring with him in private audiences, writing to him between audiences. She advised him not only on how to bring about peace with Florence but also on all the other problems that faced the Church.

Her work on behalf of Florence came to nothing, but that was not her fault, nor the pope's. He gave her full permission to negotiate a peace with Florence on terms she felt were just. But before negotiations could begin, the government in Florence changed hands. The new regime repudiated Catherine; it did not want peace — it wanted revenge.

But her trip to Avignon was not in vain; the friendship between Catherine and the pontiff — which began through their letters — developed during her four months at the papal court and became a relationship that changed the course of the Church. In their correspondence they agreed on ideas and policies. In Avignon they learned how to act to make those ideas realities.

The most urgent need in the Church was for peace: peace between the French and the English who were involved in the Hundred Years' War, peace among the states that would eventually form Italy, and peace between the papacy itself and the Republic of Florence. In addition there were three great tasks facing Gregory: to reform the clergy, to move the court back to Rome, and to launch a crusade.

Of the three, the task that excited Catherine and the pope most was the crusade. They wanted one last glorious holy war that would win back the Holy Land from the Turks and bring about the conversion of the infidels. Catherine, of course, had seen a vision in which Christians and Muslims entered together into the wound in Christ's side, washed together by His precious blood. The idea of so many nonbelievers coming to receive the grace of Jesus energized Catherine. It made her want to rush through the rest of the agenda so the crusade could be launched. It even made her, the gifted peacemaker, recommend war and the slaughter of the "infidel dogs" so other infidels could be converted.

Pope Gregory XI, a ruler and not a mystic, was interested in the crusade for other reasons. He wanted the infidels converted, of course, but he also wanted to stop the march of the Muslims westward into Christian lands. A successful crusade would establish a buffer zone, separating Christian and Muslim lands, a border area where a Christian army could be kept to protect against future invasions.

Gregory and Catherine both saw another important advantage to a holy war: it would unite the warring factions within the Church against a common foe.

Catherine believed all the great problems of the Church would disappear if only the pope would sound the call for the crusade. "Respond to the call of God, Who bids you return to the city of Saint Peter, our glorious Head," she wrote to him. "Come, and live there, and then raise the standard of the Holy Cross. This will deliver us from our wars, and divisions, and iniquities, and will at the same time convert the infidels from their errors. Then you will give good pastors to the Church, and restore her strength."[2]

Pope Gregory started to issue a call for a crusade, hesitantly and tentatively, as was always his way. One of his first acts as pontiff was to write to the rulers of Christendom (among them England, Flanders, and Venice), asking them to join him in a crusade and proposing a meeting to plan the strategy. Before the meeting took place, however, war broke out between the two strongest maritime empires, Venice and Genoa. Without ships, Gregory could launch nothing. The crusade had to be postponed until peace among the squabbling Christian factions could be established. That was in 1371.

Two years later, he called on the leaders again to meet and plan a crusade. But this call, like the earlier one, came to nothing because of wars among the Christian states.

So the pope's attention turned to the need for peace. Peace, Catherine knew, could come to the Church only if the Holy Father returned to Rome. A strong pope in Rome could restore peace to Italy; a pope in Rome could free the Church of the corruption of Avignon; a pope in Rome was where God planned him to be, and therefore was in the best position to bring Christ's grace to his Church. Gregory XI agreed on the need to return to Rome; but knowing what had to be done was not the same as doing it, not for the pope.

Catherine was a woman of courage and action. She decided what was right, then she acted. She never stopped to consider what other people might think; other people's approval or disapproval was not important to her. God's approval was all she needed.

Pope Gregory XI, by contrast, was slow to take action. He listened carefully to the opinions of others, and cared very much whether they approved or disapproved of his actions. These were among the qualities for which he was made pope, according to many historians. The French cardinals who elected him wanted the power of the papacy to stay with them, so they chose a man who would weigh their advice and want their approval.

They did not approve of a move to Rome. Gregory's predecessor, Urban V, had moved to Rome and regretted it. In May of 1367, against the advice of his French curia, Urban set out for Rome, the city of Peter. The people of Italy rejoiced. Queen Joanna I of Naples sent a fleet of ships to escort him in style. Saint John Colombini and his followers, "the little poor men of Siena," greeted him when he landed at Corneto. All along his inland route jubilant Italians, cheering and singing, ran beside the litter that carried the Holy Father. Towns and villages decorated their streets in his honor, with bright banners and garlands of flowers.

It was a great and glorious pageant, climaxed with a procession in which thousands of priests and bishops accompanied

Pope Urban V when he entered the Eternal City. But the problems the pope faced in Italy and in the Church were not solved by pageants, no matter how impressive. They were the result of years, generations, of neglect and abuse of power. They could be solved only by careful planning, bold action, and patience. The pontiff worked on them for three years, and then, discouraged at his lack of success and the continual outbreak of civil disorder, he returned to Avignon, only to die there soon thereafter.

The French cardinals who chose his successor had no desire to preside over another return of a pope to Rome. They chose from among their number a man who seemed to have extraordinary love for his family and for his native France, a quiet, timid man, who took advice well. In addition, he was a good and pious man. According to Lucius Coluzzi, who was ambassador from Florence to the court at Avignon at the time, the new pope who took the name Gregory XI was a man of blameless virtue with a reputation for "prudence, modesty, circumspection, faith, goodness, and charity; and what is yet rarer to find in a great prince, (he was renowned) for truth in his words and loyalty in his actions."[3]

The wily cardinals elected a man who was made of stronger stuff than they realized, and that man found in Catherine of Siena the ally he needed to act in the best interests of all the Church.

When Catherine visited the pope in Avignon, she saw for herself the truth she had known intuitively: that the move from Avignon was as important as it was difficult. She saw with her eyes and smelled with her nose the unbelievable depth of sin and corruption that surrounded the pope. She saw the French cardinals who advised him, encouraging him always to think first of his own great need for security, and to think next of what he could do to please his family and friends. She saw the ladies of the court, the sisters, nieces, and mistresses of the cardinals, who spent their days in gossip and intrigue, and who treated Catherine's ecstasies like spectacles to be watched, and even stuck pins in her feet to see if she could respond during an ecstasy.

Avignon was exquisitely beautiful, a masterpiece of French architecture and landscaping, a city of a thousand splendors. It is doubtful that Catherine saw any of the splendors in her four months there. Her entire being was tuned to matters of the spirit and not of the material world. Catherine told her friends that the stench of sin in Avignon sickened her.

Catherine urged the pope to leave for Rome immediately so he could get on with the other tasks of his papacy. He listened and agreed with her, then listened to his curia and agreed with them. Gregory knew what he had to do, but he found the arguments of the cardinals hard to resist, appealing as they did to his greatest fears. He asked Catherine to pray for him, after Communion, and ask Jesus to send him a sign so he would know what to do.

Catherine prayed after Communion as requested, and then became silent and rigid, rapt in prayer. When she returned to herself an hour later, those in attendance heard her murmur, "Praised be God, now and forever." Later that day Catherine wrote to Pope Gregory that God showed her no impediment to the move, and that the greatest sign he would see would be the opposition the move would continue to arouse among his courtiers.

A few days later when they were talking together, the subject of Rome came up, and he asked her, as he had so often, what she would do if she were in his position. Catherine looked long and hard at him, gazing within to read the secrets of his heart. "Who knows what ought to be done better than your Holiness, who has long since made a vow to God to return to Rome?" she asked.[4] Gregory was astonished. He had never told anyone of that promise, made so long ago. How could Catherine know about it, unless God had revealed it to her? This was the sign he had longed for. Now he was ready to act.

117

He kept his preparations secret until the last possible minute. He had ships readied to take him to Genoa, and from there to Rome. Catherine, who stayed in Avignon until his departure, did not sail with him, but traveled by land, stopping in Genoa to rest before continuing on to Siena.

Before the pope left on this momentous trip that meant so much to the Church, his family and advisers tried one more time to change his mind. His father, an old man and ailing, threw himself across the threshold of the palace gate, blocking the way as Gregory tried to leave. "How can my son so coldly forsake not only his country but even his old father? Well, then, before he departs, he shall pass over my body!"[5] The pope stepped over his father and made his way down to the waiting ships.

The sea voyage was a disaster. Gregory's little fleet was buffeted by storms and marooned for a time on a deserted island. Finally, sick and weary, the entourage reached the harbor at Genoa. The cardinals, of course, wanted to return to France as soon as the vessels were seaworthy again. They had heard rumors that the Florentines were planning to kill the pope, and other rumors that the magistrates of Rome would not welcome him. Pope Gregory began to think they were right about turning back, but he wanted to talk to Catherine before he made his decision.

She and her party had traveled by land and reached Genoa a few days earlier. They were comfortably housed with a devout woman named Orietta Scotta, resting and gathering strength for the rest of their trip.

Though they were in the same city, it was not easy for them to meet. The pope did not want her to come to his ship because the cardinals would find out. On the other hand, he could not visit her because of the crowds. All day long the street in front of her house was full of people, the faithful and the curious, the devout and the desperate, hoping the saint of Siena would come out and bless them. It would not be right for a pope to have to shove his way through a crowd. Many people did, of course. There was a steady stream of visitors forcing its way to see Catherine. Doctors, lawyers, magistrates: all the important people of Genoa were coming to meet the holy woman.

In the end Gregory disguised himself as a humble priest and stole out at night, alone, to visit her. Even then there were a lot of people on the Via del Canneto. Small groups, huddled about fires; other groups praying quietly. No one noticed as the pope walked by, making his way to Catherine's door.

Catherine prayed with the Holy Father that night in Genoa. A note written in the margin of her secretary's journal for the date says, "This prayer was made at Genoa by the said virgin, to dissuade Pope Gregory from the project of returning [to Avignon]; things contrary to the journey to Rome having been deliberated on in the Consistory."

The prayer, too, has been preserved. It goes: "O Eternal God, permit not that Thy Vicar should yield to the counsels of the flesh, nor judge according to the senses and self-love, nor that he suffer himself to be terrified by any opposition. O Immortal Love! If Thou art offended by his hesitations and delays, punish them on my body which I offer to Thee to be tormented and destroyed according to Thy will and pleasure."[6]

That was the last meeting between Catherine and Gregory XI, though they continued to correspond as long as he lived. She stayed on in Genoa for a month because of illness among members of her party. As soon as his ships were ready, he set sail for Rome where he was received with great joy and celebration, not only by the Romans themselves, but by the bishops and priests and leading citizens of all the surrounding area, who yearned for peace and order and believed the pope could provide them.

Gregory's reign in Rome never did bring peace. Though he made generous overtures to the Florentines, he did not reach agreement with them. He became disheartened, surrounded as he was with unhappy advisers, living in a land where he did not understand the language or the customs. He did not know where to begin on the reform of the Church that he knew was so necessary. He died in March of 1378, just a year and a half after he left Avignon. The one great accomplishment of his papacy was the move to Rome. Even that soon proved to be a mixed blessing.

9

Catherine's Last Agony

Catherine was in Florence when she received the news of Pope Gregory XI's death. Her friend, her "dear Babbo," was in heaven now, with Jesus and all the saints. She yearned to be there with them.

She felt a stabbing hunger to receive our Lord in the Blessed Sacrament. But there was no Holy Eucharist in Florence; there was no Mass. Instead there was papal interdict, locked churches, excommunication. "Dear Babbo" had not accomplished all he hoped to do when he left Avignon. He left a lot of unfinished business for his successor. Catherine wondered who would be chosen to succeed him.

All Christendom wondered who would be chosen. The citizens of Rome in particular wondered who would be chosen. They wanted one of their own, a man they could understand, a man they could trust. They had had enough of these foreign popes. They wanted a Roman this time. They took to the streets with their message, chanting and shouting their need for a Roman pope. Soon they were rioting, running up and down the streets like madmen, carrying clubs, looking for victims.

It was exactly what the French cardinals had feared all

along: Rome was not a safe place. The Romans could not be trusted. How could the curia elect a new pope under these conditions? What could they do? They could not leave the city because the streets were not safe, especially for French cardinals; for the same reason, their colleagues who were out of town could not join them. They could not delay their meeting either. The Church needed a pope.

In this atmosphere of fear and mistrust, the cardinals in Rome met to choose a new pontiff. They did not pick a Roman, but neither did they choose a Frenchman. Instead they elected a native of Naples, Bartolomeo Prignano, archbishop of Bari. He took the name Urban VI.

The cardinals were afraid to tell the people what they had done. They did not know what those "barbarous" Romans might do, so they started a rumor that Cardinal Tebaldeschi of Saint Peter's, a favorite in the city, had been elected pope but declined the honor because of his age. Their ruse failed. When the mob heard that Tebaldeschi had been elected, they did not stay to hear the rest of the message. In great joy they rushed to the old man's residence, seized him, and dressed him in papal robes. When they learned their mistake, they were enraged. Insisting that they did not want the archbishop of Bari, a Neapolitan, for a pope, they cried: "We want none but a Roman!"

In a few days the city calmed down. Urban VI was duly installed as pope in the church of Saint John Lateran, and started on the unfinished work of his predecessor: restoration of peace and reform of the clergy. But the seeds of schism had already been sown by the lies spoken in fear that night.

When the news reached Catherine that the archbishop of Bari had been made pope, she was elated. She had met him in Avignon and had been impressed by him as a man of penance. He despised the sin and luxury of Avignon as much as she did. He lived austerely, and believed that all priests should. He would be quite a contrast to the popes of recent years, Catherine thought. And he was a man who did not care about the opinions of others. That, too, would provide a pleasant contrast with his predecessor.

She wondered how he felt about the crusade. Being from Naples he would have the backing of Queen Joanna I, who had a powerful army and an impressive fleet of ships. They could be the beginning of a great army that could go out in the name of the Church to win back the Holy Land.

Catherine wrote to friends in Lecceto and shared her enthusiasm for the new pope, assuring them that he would be "a good and just pastor, who is resolved to purge and root up vices, and to plant virtues; fearing no one and acting justly and bravely."[1]

More news about Pope Urban VI came to Catherine in a letter from her friend Dom Bartholomew. "He shows great confidence in God; and on that account fears no man in the world, and openly proclaims his resolve to banish the simonies and pomps that reign in the Church of God, and himself shows the example by living moderately with all his court," he wrote, confirming what Catherine already believed about the man.

The letter also had some references to the peace Catherine was trying to negotiate: "He says he will have peace, but with the honor of the holy Church; that he does not care for money, and that the Florentines must come to him with truth, and not with lies."[2]

Catherine liked most of the news about Urban VI, especially the part about his wanting peace with the Florentines and the honor of the Church. But there was no mention of mercy for Florence in any of the reports. Mercy and compassion, Catherine felt, were essential to true peace.

She wrote to the new pope as she had written so often to his predecessor, urging him to show fatherly forgiveness to the disobedient Florentines. "Give them the good of bringing them back into the fold," she urged, "and if they do not ask for it in true and perfect humility, let your Holiness fulfill their imperfection. Receive from a sick man what he can give you. Oh me! oh me! have mercy on so many souls that perish!"[3]

"Mingle mercy with justice," she urged, "lest your justice become unjust." But Pope Urban VI did not listen, not to Catherine, nor to anyone else. He proved to have all the good qualities Dom Bartholomew and Catherine hoped for in him; but he lacked a sense of mercy. Leniency and compromise were either not known to him, or simply not respected. They certainly were not practiced. Neither was tact.

The day after his coronation, at the conclusion of Vespers, Urban denounced some of the bishops present, accusing them of lying when they said they had to be in Rome. Their proper place, he declared, was not at the papal court but at home with their flocks. The bishops were outraged, both by the idea that they should leave Rome and by being publicly reprimanded.

A few days later, the new pope took on the cardinals, calling them together, and reading them the Gospel of the Good Shepherd, then telling them with startling clarity exactly where they were failing.

In a short time Pope Urban alienated most of the powerful men in the Church. He had never had a strong power base, being neither French nor a cardinal. He had the backing of Queen Joanna I of Naples, but not for long. When Otto of Brunswick, Joanna's third husband (her fourth, according to certain historians), came to congratulate him on his election, the pope was rude and insulting to him. To add insult to injury, Urban opposed the marriage of one of Joanna's kinsmen to the daughter of the king of Sicily, which enraged both royal families. On the subject of peace between England and France, a peace his predecessors had tried in vain to negotiate, he let it be known before talks started that he intended to win justice for the English, thus driving the French even further from him.

Catherine had known that the pope was a strong-willed

man who disregarded the opinions of others, but she did not know that he would alienate so many people so quickly. She wrote to him about mercy and forgiveness. She pleaded with him to arrange a peace with Florence and lift the interdict. She had vowed that she would not abandon Florence until there was peace. She would not break that promise, but she yearned to leave the city. She missed Siena and her circle of friends. She had made converts in Florence, friends who were as loyal to her as any in Siena, and she had visitors from home. Still it was not the same.

Raymond of Capua was in Rome, in the middle of all the excitement and turmoil. Catherine was in Florence in the middle of the interdict and she hated it. Spring was turning to summer and she was still in Florence.

In June, just two months after Urban's coronation, the French cardinals went to the resort city of Agnani to avoid the heat of Rome. They wrote to the Holy Father asking him to meet with them there. They wanted to persuade him to resign. He refused their invitation. The cardinals countered by circulating rumors that his election was invalid because those who voted were in fear of their lives at the time.

The other cardinals, the Spanish, and even the Italians, sided with the French in this dispute. Only one — old Cardinal Tebaldeschi, who was on his deathbed — remained loyal to Pope Urban VI, but he died soon after denouncing what the other cardinals were doing.

Catherine was horrified by these rumors and the disloyalty of the cardinals. Urban was a difficult man, she conceded, but he was still the pope. "Even if he were the devil incarnate," she had always said, "we should not raise our heads against him because he is sweet Christ on earth." She spent her nights writing letters urging people to be loyal to Pope Urban. That summer, after the long-awaited peace treaty was signed and she returned to Siena, she continued to send letters to people all over Europe, reminding them of their duty to "sweet Christ on earth." But things were getting worse, not better, for the Church and the pope.

In September, Pope Urban VI named twenty-six new cardinals, his own friends, all but two of them Italian. The Agnani cardinals met again, demanding that the Holy Father appear before them. When he refused, they denounced him as a usurper and an anti-Christ. They wrote a letter to this effect, which they sent to all the heads of state in Europe.

Then they elected a new pope, Cardinal Count Robert of Geneva, who took the name Clement VII. Robert was a soldier as well as a cardinal, one of the cruelest men the French ever sent to serve the Church in Italy. He once led a group of Breton mercenaries in a massacre at Cesena. At the time of Urban's election he had ten thousand of those same Breton troops poised, ready to invade Florence. Under the inappropriate name of Clement VII, he and his cardinals moved back to Avignon and announced his election to the world.

The Great Western Schism that Catherine had foreseen before she ever left for Avignon, had taken place. The antipope, with his cardinals who were so skilled in the use of power, sat in France. Pope Urban VI — hot-tempered, rigid, unpleasant — sat in Rome. The faithful were in the desperate position of having to decide which pope to follow.

For Catherine there was no choice. Urban was properly elected and therefore had her loyalty. Many in the Church did not agree with her. Queen Joanna I of Naples backed the pope in Avignon and, not surprisingly, so did the king of France. A dismaying number of heads of state chose Avignon over Rome.

Urban VI recognized Catherine's loyalty. He wanted her to come to Rome, to be his ambassador to Queen Joanna. Raymond of Capua, who was still in Rome, passed on this request. Catherine had only just returned from Florence. She wanted to be in Rome with Raymond and the Holy Father, but she knew that many people in Siena would be angry if she left again so soon. Catherine wrote back that she would go to

Rome only if the pontiff himself asked her. Then she would have to do it under "holy obedience," and everyone would understand that.

Pope Urban personally wrote to Catherine, asking her to come to Rome. She agreed and made her plans. This was not going to be an easy trip for her. She realized it would probably be her last trip. The pain and weakness grew worse each day. Although she was quite sure she had the strength to walk to Rome, she did not know about the trip back.

On a cool, crisp day in November, 1378, Catherine set out for Rome with a small band of close friends, perhaps twenty-five in all, who wanted to make the difficult trip with her.

This was a pilgrimage for the Church. The friends carried no food and no money, planning to beg, like true pilgrims. They dressed simply, in the homespun of their various religious orders, and wore sandals on their feet. Alessia Saracini was part of the troop; so was Lisa, Catherine's sister-in-law, and faithful Cecca, and several other members of the Mantellate.

There were men in the group, too, of course: Neri di Landoccio, the melancholy poet, and his friend Gabriele Piccolomini, who would serve as secretaries; Father Bartholomew Dominic, who was always with her making note of everything that happened. Father John Tantucci was there, the Augustinian who, years before, had questioned her theology and stayed to be a disciple; so was the hermit Santi in whose hermitage she wrote parts of *The Dialogue*. There were other priests, too, and monks.

Their hearts were heavy as they set out. This was not a pleasant romp through the fields they were undertaking, but a hard, potentially dangerous journey to a war-torn foreign city where more danger and hardship awaited them, and where they would work and pray and sacrifice for a Church that was riddled with corruption and torn by schism, under the leadership of an irascible, possibly irrational, man: Pope Urban VI.

But they made the trip gladly because they made it with Catherine, their "beloved Mama." No sacrifice was too great, no trip too dangerous, as long as they were with her.

The citizens of Siena lined the streets to say good-bye to their beloved saint. Many wept openly, believing that they would never see Catherine again, that she would never have the strength to return from this mission to Rome. They followed her out through the city gate and along the road that led to Rome, wanting to be with her as long as they could.

Some of Catherine's very dearest and closest friends were not able to make the trip. Monna Lapa and Stephen Maconi, to name just two, wanted to go with her, but for reasons of health and business could not make the trip. They wept inconsolably at the separation and then took care of their business so they could join her in Rome as soon as possible.

The pilgrims walked slowly, resting often for Catherine's sake. They looked forward to seeing Raymond again. It had been months since they had seen him. Catherine missed him terribly. She offered that suffering and all the suffering of the pilgrimage as a loving sacrifice for the sake of the Church; and as she walked she pleaded with God to heal the schism, to give the cardinals in Avignon the grace to see their sin.

Catherine arrived in Rome on the first Sunday of Advent in 1378. Two days later she met with Pope Urban VI, reassuring him of her loyalty and that of her followers. The Holy Father needed her reassurance. He was a beleaguered man, afraid for his own life, and the life of the Church. Breton troops roamed the streets. The pope and his cardinals seldom ventured outside the papal apartments and seldom allowed outsiders to come in. They lived in a constant state of fear.

The pope asked Catherine to address his curia. Father Bartholomew Dominic described what happened to Urban when he heard Catherine speak. She made a short formal speech reminding them all that their faith was in our Lord Jesus Christ, whose power for good has no limits, and urging them to have courage, not based on their own power, but on that of Christ.

When she finished, Pope Urban said, "This little woman puts us all to shame. We are troubled and afraid, while she, who belongs by nature to the timid sex, is fearless; she even gives us others consolation." Then after a moment's pause for reflection, he started in again with a new tone in his voice and a new and happier look in his face: "What can the Viceregent fear when Christ the Almighty is with him? Christ is stronger than the world, and it cannot be that He will fail His Holy Church!"[4]

Urban VI found, as so many others had, that he was braver and better when he was with Catherine. He changed his mind about sending her to Naples, but insisted that she stay with him in Rome. Ever obedient, Catherine and her friends stayed. She continued to meet with the Holy Father and to write to various heads of state and princes of the Church, urging them to unite behind Urban.

In Rome Catherine saw Raymond of Capua again. That reunion was joyful, especially for Catherine who still found Raymond to be the only human who really understood her, the only true companion to her soul she had ever met.

But in December, 1378, just two weeks after Catherine arrived in Rome, Urban sent Raymond on a mission to France to persuade King Charles that he should support him, Urban VI, and not the antipope in Avignon, Clement VII. The trip offered little hope of success, and much danger. Catherine, who yearned for a martyr's death, would have relished such an assignment. Raymond, man of moderation, did not. He accepted the assignment reluctantly and pursued it only as far as Genoa. There he heard rumors that the schismatics were plotting to capture him. He decided to stay in Genoa. He worked with the Dominicans there and soon became the head of that province.

Catherine was shocked by what she perceived as Raymond's cowardice. She wrote to him often while he was in Genoa. At first she wrote of little besides his need for courage, and the glory of martyrdom. Later she was able to turn to other subjects, eventually pouring out her soul freely to him once more as she described the slow approach of death with its physical and spiritual agony. They never met again after Raymond failed in his mission as ambassador to France; and one of the great sufferings she had to bear was the loneliness of facing death without her great listener there to share each moment with her.

Catherine and the pope called for a new crusade, a spiritual crusade against the evil forces, the powers and principalities that were attacking the Church. They asked all the faithful to pray and fast for a victory over these evil powers, and they asked that they to come to Rome, to rally in support of their Holy Father. Many came. Many used Catherine's house as a rendezvous place. As many as one hundred people at a time stayed with Catherine, accepting her hospitality, praying, fasting, and suffering with her for the healing of the Church.

Conditions in Rome improved somewhat. Fighting in the streets stopped. The Breton forces were driven out of town, and the pope was able to walk from his residence in exile, through the streets of Rome, to Saint Peter's. But the schism was not healed and true peace was not restored in the Church. There was less and less communication between Catherine and Pope Urban VI. He was alienated from everyone, alone, angry, isolated.

And she was growing weaker. When she could, she dragged herself to Saint Peter's to attend Mass and spend the rest of the day in prayer there. More and more often she was not able even to leave her bed.

The new year of 1380 arrived, and with it the time for Catherine's last great act of love and sacrifice for the Church. Catherine had known suffering all of her life; she had embraced suffering as her refreshment because her Beloved, her

Savior, had embraced suffering. But in the last months of her life she entered into a new realm of the mystery of suffering.

Her body gave every appearance of being ready for death. All of her friends expected her to die within the hour. She herself yearned for death, and union with her Beloved. But she agreed not to die, and to accept instead an additional period of agony, for the sake of the Church. As an extra penance she refrained from drinking water.

Near the end of this ordeal of suffering, as her strength ebbed away, her friends heard her cry out, "O Eternal God, accept the sacrifice of my life for the mystical body of Thy holy Church. I have nothing to give save that which Thou hast given to me. Take my heart then, and press it out over the face of Thy Spouse!" And she saw God do that, taking her heart from her body and squeezing it out over the Church.[5]

Catherine's mission to the Church was the major work of her life. She did other things, it is true. She wrote a book that is considered a classic. She had good friends. She brought healing and conversion of heart to many souls. And, of course, she had her own wonderful relationship with God. But the great work, the work for which she was called and trained by God, the work that occupied most of her energy and prayer during her mature years, had to do with fighting corruption in the Church.

Most people who examine the record conclude that despite heroic efforts, Catherine did not succeed. But she herself felt otherwise. As she lay on her bed, waiting for death and watching God squeeze her heart out over the Church, she cried out, "Thanks, thanks be to the Most High, the Eternal, Who has placed us like knights on a field of battle to [take part in] combat for His Spouse, protected by the shield of holy faith. THE FIELD IS WON! THE VICTORY IS OURS!"[6]

As long as she had breath in her, Catherine continued to pray for the Church and to instruct her companions. She told each of them what they should do after her death. Stephen

Maconi was to become a Carthusian, for instance. Others were to join other orders. Raymond of Capua was to keep a fatherly eye on all of them.

She gazed at the crucifix for hours on end. "Blood, blood, blood," she whispered from time to time, contemplating Christ's great act of love till the very end. At last, on Sunday, April 29, 1380, surrounded by loving friends and her mother, Catherine spoke her last words. "Blood, blood, blood," she groaned, followed by, "Father, into Thy hands I commend my spirit."" And then she died.

10

After Her Death

Throughout Catherine's life, it seemed, miracles flowed to her and from her. After her death the miracles continued. Those who were especially close to her, but could not be present at the moment of her death, Raymond of Capua among others, reported that she personally came and announced her passing to them. When her body was put on display for her mourners, thousands upon thousands of people filed through the church to honor her and to seek healing through her intercession.

Despite the fact that no one had announced Catherine's death or organized a concourse, and that her friends had been at pains to keep the matter of her death secret, "The whole population of Rome gathered swiftly at the church where her body lay awaiting burial," Raymond wrote. The crowds that came began reverently to kiss her hands and feet, and to commend themselves to her prayers. So great was the throng that it was found necessary to place Catherine's body behind the iron grating of the chapel of Saint Dominic.

"Already among these crowds there were some who, believing firmly in the merits of Catherine's sanctity, brought with them their sick or their disabled, in order to petition their cure from the Lord in virtue of her merits. Nor were they disappointed. . . ."[1] Raymond goes on to detail story after story

133

of miraculous cures and healings that were attributed to Catherine after her death.

It was the custom of the day to dismember the corpse of a holy person so that the various parts could be venerated and used in connection with prayers for healing. The great cathedrals of the time had special rooms in which these body parts were kept as relics, each in its own beautiful custom-made container. The forearm of a saint, for instance, might have an ornately carved silver case, like an incredibly beautiful silver glove. Other parts might be housed in urns or boxes carved from gemstones, or mounted in an arrangement of crystal and gold.

Stephen Maconi thought that this should be done with Catherine's body. Of all her companions, Stephen suffered most without her. As long as her body remained on view in the chapel of Saint Dominic, he stayed beside it. After her funeral he stayed with her casket, weeping over it by day and sleeping on it at night. The time came for him to leave Rome, but he had great difficulty making that break. He thought it would be easier if he could take part of Catherine with him. He consulted with Alessia and some of the others. And then, "with great reverence," he removed a tooth, and then a second tooth, which he gave to Alessia, and a third for Neri di Landoccio, which they all treasured as their most prized possessions and used to bring about the healing of many diseases.

Other parts of her body were removed at other times. Mother Theodosia Drane, as quoted earlier, saw one of Catherine's hands preserved in a convent in Rome, and reported that another could be seen in Semignano.

It was the wish of all of Catherine's followers that her body, or at least her head, could return to Siena, to be venerated there. Father Raymond of Capua, after he was elected superior general of the Dominican Order in 1380, received papal permission to carry out this plan. He had the head removed from the body and placed in a silk bag for the trip home. Then he had a reliquary of gilded copper prepared and placed in the sacristy of San Domenico. On the appointed day in spring, a solemn procession — which included her mother, all of her devoted followers, and most of the citizens of Siena — formally brought the cherished head to its chosen place of honor to be venerated and to continue to be a source of comfort and healing for those who love Catherine.

PART TWO

□

Catherine Now

11

The Real Miracle: Catherine Herself

When the general chapter of the Dominicans met in Florence in 1374, its members questioned Catherine and sought answers to two major concerns. First, what was her doctrine and how did she learn it? Second, was she really going without food, and if so by what power? These same questions absorbed Raymond of Capua when he wrote her biography. He devoted page after page to careful consideration of these two issues. Even today, the same questions must be considered by anyone who struggles to understand the complex and singular woman who was Catherine of Siena.

Her doctrine has been scrutinized by the Church in recent years, and the official conclusions — as proclaimed by Pope Paul VI and Pope John Paul II — will be discussed in the next chapter. Their statements, however, concentrate on her writings; they do not explore her way of life: her fasting, self-mortification, and ecstasies — those outward signs of holiness that were so fascinating to the people of her day and ours.

Lay scholars have been less reluctant to write about these aspects of Catherine's story. Of particular interest are the writings of Rudolph Bell, Dr. Hilde Bruch, and others who study eating disorders. They have examined Catherine's writings, the biographies written by her friends, and the biographies of other saints of the period. They have concluded that many holy women, including Saint Catherine, probably lived for months, even years, without eating anything but the Eucharist, as their followers claimed.

These long-term fasts were not the work of Satan, according to these writers, but they were not necessarily the work of God either. God's grace may have abounded in the women's lives, but their fasts appear to have been the work of the women themselves. Their minds and bodies, dwelling always on self-denial, self-mortification, and the destruction of self-will, produced a kind of anorexia. (The word comes from the Greek and means "loss of appetite.")

"Holy anorexia" is the term Bell uses to describe the disease that developed in holy women of the Middle Ages who sought an ideal of sanctity, and he distinguishes their disorder from anorexia nervosa, a disease found in the twentieth century among young women seeking an ideal of thinness and feminine beauty. In a recent book entitled *Holy Anorexia*, Bell describes two styles of holiness that were followed by hundreds, perhaps thousands, of young women during the Middle Ages. Both styles included severe dietary restrictions and both sometimes resulted in anorexia.

The first style, and by far the most attractive to the women of the day, was that of Saint Clare of Assisi. Bell describes her as the first saint whose anorexia can be traced through official documents. In the investigation that led to her beatification, the Sisters who lived with Clare at San Damiano were questioned concerning her eating habits. They told the interrogators that for many years she observed a total fast on Mondays, Wednesdays, and Fridays, and ate very little on the other days of the week. This pattern of diet may have developed in her childhood, long before she ran away from home to live the kind of holy life Saint Francis had chosen. This severe and prolonged fast took its toll on Clare's body, leaving her emaciated, weak, and eventually unable to get out of bed. Francis, no stranger to austerities, intervened and ordered her to eat at least an ounce and a half of bread each day. Clare obeyed, recovered, and in time wrote a rule for her religious order that called for moderate austerity in the matter of diet.

Clare's spirituality, of course, included more than dietary restrictions. Like Saint Francis, she put great emphasis on vows of chastity, poverty, and obedience. She wore no shoes, slept on the ground, kept silence whenever possible, and never left the monastery. The utter simplicity of this life, which contrasted so sharply with the home life of affluent families of the day, attracted hundreds of young women of Tuscany. A few of them continued to live at home, observing their vows privately, but most joined convents of Poor Clares where they lived prayerfully among their sisters. In many of these women, as in Clare herself, there was a tendency to fast too rigorously and to slip into irreversible anorexia. This was often prevented by their vow of obedience and their communal life whose rule was based on Clare's experience in fasting. Obedience to the rule saved many Sisters from dietary extremes just as Clare's obedience to Francis had saved her.

The other style of female holiness developed within the Dominican tradition. The Dominican women did not imitate a single, popular saint like Clare. Many of the Dominican women were loners. They lived at home, connecting themselves to other Dominicans only very loosely, often through the Third Order, the Mantellate. But they lived lives of religious intensity that went far beyond the demands of that order. They worked out their spirituality alone, without the benefit of the close companionship of peers, or the accumulated wisdom of an order to moderate their lives. Most important, they did not submit themselves to an authority they lived with, one who could see firsthand how they lived. The vow of obedience that protected the Poor Clares could not protect these more individualistic holy women because the authorities to whom they vowed obedience, their confessors and bishops, knew only what the holy women told them about their lives. They were strong-willed women, determined to submit their wills to the will of God and convinced that the way to do this was through self-mortification and fasting. Many became anorectic and died painful deaths by starvation.

Catherine's life followed the model of the holy Dominican loner. She sought heroic holiness, and saw fasting and physical suffering as a means to that end. By refusing to marry and by joining the Mantellate instead of a convent, she lived outside the scrutiny of authorities and away from the moderating influence a community might have provided. Her fasting and self-denial went unchecked, developed into anorexia, and brought about her eventual death by starvation.

To view Saint Catherine as a holy anorectic who followed a pattern common to other holy anorectics seems harsh and unloving because it is empty of all mention of the Holy Spirit whose fruits were so evident in Catherine. Yet an examination of anorexia, including the part it may have played in her life, is necessary to an understanding of how God worked in her life.

This examination also affirms the accuracy of accounts written by those who loved her. Raymond of Capua, Bartholomew Dominic, Tommaso Caffarini, and all the others were so accurate that the symptoms and progress of her disease can be traced through their writings. Bell says he was first drawn to the idea of holy anorexia because the biographies of holy women of the Middle Ages and the depositions regarding them were strikingly similar to the clinical records of twentieth-century anorectics.

Though anorexia has been around for hundreds of years, it has only recently been named and studied. It is not so thoroughly understood that a definitive list of symptoms can be given. Yet some description of the disorder can be made.

Anorexia is a disease with psychological as well as physical aspects. At the very heart of the disease is a struggle of wills. Typically it begins as a woman tries to assert her independence, but is pressured by her father or husband to conform to the roles defined for her by society. (In Catherine's case, the pressure came through her mother, but the conflict was, nevertheless, between the role Catherine chose for herself and the role society chose for her.)

As the struggle for freedom and control rages, the young woman who cannot control society, or her family, or even her own life, becomes preoccupied with controlling her body, through fasting or diet. If the struggle goes on long enough and if the fasting is extreme, anorexia develops. The woman stops wanting to eat. Unless there is intervention at this point, as there was in Saint Clare's life, she becomes unable to eat, unable to retain food in her stomach, unable to digest. In the end, then, she loses control of her body to anorexia, and eventually she starves to death.

Ninety percent of anorectics are female, and most are under the age of twenty-five. But the disease does not develop unless there is a struggle for control. Saint Clare was a typical candidate for the disease. Her family insisted that she marry; she insisted that she did not want to marry. Eventually she ran away from home to live a life of simplicity and holiness. She chose a life of rigorous fasting to achieve great holiness, but seems to have lost control over her fasting until Saint Francis intervened. It is interesting that Francis may have fasted more rigorously than she, but was not in danger of anorexia. Because he was a male, he was free to control his life in a way that Clare could not. Francis remained free to stop his fasts; Clare very nearly lost the ability to stop. Many other young women, seeking holiness through fasting, did lose that ability.

The disease has several phases: there is usually an early period of introversion, characterized by preoccupation with the fast or the diet and control of the body; later there is usually a period of great activity and cheerfulness and, often, strenuous exercise programs; finally, there is a time of weakness and pain, and, unless the patient can be induced to eat, starvation results.

These phases can easily be seen in Catherine's life. First came the years of seclusion in her cell where she fought so hard against self-will and indulgence. Then came the phase of great physical activity when she came out of seclusion. She astounded people with her cheerfulness and her boundless energy, though she ate almost nothing. She did the work of the maid around the house, for instance, and many other chores besides; she worked around the clock during the plague; she traveled throughout Siena on her errands of mercy. But eventually she moved into the last phase of the disease, when eating had become impossible; pain and weakness were constant; even getting out of bed was often out of the question for her.

All of these phases overlap somewhat. Catherine at times was so weak and full of pain she could hardly drag herself from bed. "Miraculously" she would find the energy to do an arduous work of charity, but then the weakness would return.

Most anorectics are preoccupied with food, thinking of it all the time. Many find satisfaction in cooking and serving others. Some even become overbearing about it, insisting that their families eat the huge meals they long for themselves. Here, too, we find Catherine following the pattern. She enjoyed cooking for her family and serving them, but not eating with them. In time of famine she baked bread for the hungry, all day long, day after day, but she did not eat any of it herself.

Bulimia (binge eating usually followed by vomiting) may be associated with the disease in its early stages. By the time full suppression of appetite has taken place, however, any amount of food can induce vomiting. Most anorectics become expert at making themselves vomit. Catherine is said to have used a long twig that she forced down her throat. Other holy anorectics preferred a feather.

There is no evidence that Catherine ever indulged in

binge eating, but she did think of herself as a glutton. In a letter to a priest who believed that her fasting was inspired by Satan and should be stopped, she pointed out that through this special grace God was correcting in her the sin of gluttony which she had been unable to correct in herself.

Many anorectics suffer a physical trauma that contributes to the disease. Bell thinks that the incident in which Catherine forced herself to drink the bowl of pus from Andrea's wound, as related earlier, may have been the trauma in her life. Raymond of Capua wrote that after that incident she had a vision in which she drank blood from the side of Christ and never needed earthly food again.

One of the most interesting aspects of anorexia, for those who seek to understand the spirituality of medieval saints, is that its victims come to perceive pain as pleasure. Dr. Bruch, who runs a clinic for anorectics and wrote *The Golden Cage: The Enigma of Anorexia Nervosa*, reports that her young patients "brainwash" themselves about pain. When they first start dieting, they learn to think of hunger as something good because it will make them thin. They come to think of hunger, then, as desirable, and eventually reach a point where they find pleasure in the pain of hunger. Some patients told Dr. Bruch that having reached that stage, they found all pain pleasurable.

That phenomenon sheds light on some of Catherine's statements about pain. When she received the stigmata, for instance, she found the pain unbearable, so excruciating that she lost consciousness. She was sure she would die within days, feeling the agony of the nails. But a week to the day after that pain began she told Raymond, ". . . those wounds no longer cause it (my body) pain, but rather lend it force and vigor. I can feel strength flowing into me from those wounds which at first only added to my sufferings."[1]

Many of Catherine's statements about pain, and indeed her whole attitude toward pain, take on new meaning in the light of what Dr. Bruch reports about anorectics and pain. Catherine once told her friend Alessia, for example, "I wish pains to be food to me, tears my drink, sweat my ointment. Let pains make me fat, let pains cure me, let pains give me light, let pains give me wisdom, let pains clothe my nakedness, let pains strip me of all self-love."[2]

She wrote a letter to Sister Bartolomea della Seta in which she made some astounding statements about pain. "This is the state of the perfect," she wrote. "If it were possible for them to escape Hell, and have joy in this life and joy eternal beside, they do not want it, because they delight so greatly in conforming themselves to Christ crucified; nay, they want to live rather by the way of the Cross and pain, than without pain." Later in the same letter she wrote, "I do not avoid pains, for I have chosen pains for my refreshment." And again, "I would rather exert myself for Christ crucified, feeling pain, gloom and inward conflicts, than not exert myself and feel repose."[3]

Another characteristic that Dr. Bruch found in many of her patients was a heightened sensitivity to all sensory stimuli. For example, colors seemed brighter, sounds louder. Some women found this so troublesome that they preferred to stay awake at night, because there were fewer sounds and less light to bother them. Here, too, there is a parallel in Catherine's life.

Anorectics in the late stages of their disease have a lot in common with people who suffer from starvation. The big difference between the two conditions is that the person who is starving, not of his own volition, will eat if food is presented, whereas the anorectic will not. The mental disorders reported by victims of starvation — the distortions of perception, visions, hallucinations — are also common among anorectics. No one who loved Catherine would want to think of her as having hallucinations. On the other hand, no one would deny that she tended to have unusual visual perceptions.

There does seem to be, then, considerable evidence linking Catherine with anorexia. She could easily have slipped into a pattern of fasting that eventually would take control of her. All of the major ingredients of the anorectic life were present: the overpowering presence of a parent who demanded conformity to society's choices for her; the conviction that fasting and suffering would lead her to the greatest achievement possible for a human, union with Jesus; total lack of guidance from anyone whose authority she respected — until it was too late.

The case for Catherine's anorexia has not been proven with absolute certainty. But to this observer at least, it is the most plausible explanation for Saint Catherine's prolonged fasting. This explanation has the additional advantage of making her attitude toward pain more understandable. And it makes the stories of her boundless energy sound more believable.

Does this mean Catherine was "merely" anorectic, instead of saintly and holy? Not at all. The evidence seems to indicate that she was both anorectic and holy. Like many saints before her and after her she had a fatal disease, and that disease had a powerful effect on the way she lived during the last years of her life. But the disease never caused her to abandon God; nor did it cause Him to abandon her.

Saint Thérèse of Lisieux, the much-loved Little Flower, suffered from tuberculosis. But she was not *merely* tubercular, instead of saintly and holy: she was both tubercular and holy. She gave herself wholeheartedly to God before she contracted tuberculosis, and continued to give herself to God as she suffered and died of tuberculosis.

In the same way, Catherine lived a holy life, serving God as generously as she knew how, before her anorexia developed, and continued to live that way after it developed.

Anorexia did not cause Catherine's holiness; neither did it destroy it. Neither did it, by itself, prove her holiness.

Anorexia was one element in a life that had many extraordinary and powerful elements.

If anorexia were the only power at work in Catherine's life, then any one of Dr. Bruch's anorectic patients could experience the beatific vision or write a treatise on prayer like *The Dialogue*. There was a lot more to Catherine than anorexia. There was her enormous love for Jesus and her willingness to obey Him. There was His even more enormous love for her, and His grace, which He poured into her life with such generosity.

Catherine's love for God permeated every moment of her life, opening her heart and her mind to His will, giving her the courage to obey Him in all things. His love for her and His grace in her life enlightened her mind and transformed her deeds into acts with permanent spiritual value for all the world.

Any anorectic might have hallucinations and distorted visual perceptions, but only a soul committed to God would be open to receiving divine revelations; and only God's grace could transform a tendency to hallucinate into the rich prayer life Catherine enjoyed. Any anorectic might suffer great pain. Only someone who knew and shared God's love for mankind could turn that suffering into a willing sacrifice for the salvation of souls. Any anorectic might have periods of tremendous energy. Only one who took the Gospel seriously would use that energy to care for God's needy.

The real miracle of Catherine's life, then, was not that she went for years without eating; that, as it turns out, was almost commonplace in the Middle Ages. Bell lists two hundred sixty-one possible holy anorectics, whose names are found in the *Bibliotheca Sanctorum* and who lived in the regions of Lombardy and Tuscany alone. Other scholars have studied holy anorectics of other geographic regions. Nor was the real miracle the way she withstood the abuse she forced her body to endure. Many have suffered worse and lived.

The real miracle of Catherine's life was the depth of love that flowed between her and God. Her desire to please Him dominated her life and opened the way for a continual flow of His grace into her life, perfecting and completing her humanity. That is the real miracle and the real source of sanctity in the life of Saint Catherine of Siena.

12

Doctor of the Church

On October 4, 1970, in a solemn ceremony in Saint Peter's Basilica in Rome, Pope Paul VI proclaimed Catherine of Siena a Doctor of the Church. She was radically different from those who had previously received this title. She was a woman. (The only other female to be honored in this way was Saint Theresa of Ávila.) She was a lay person; other Doctors of the Church have held high position in important ecclesial organizations. Most striking of all, she was uneducated and almost illiterate.

Catherine's humble background and lack of education may have made her an unlikely candidate for such an honor, but they never hindered her ability to receive divine revelation. In fact, God has so consistently revealed His word to the poor and the humble that, as Paul VI put it, we can consider them to be "God's preferential choice."

This tradition is older than Christianity itself. God chose the descendants of Abraham, an otherwise insignificant little band of Semites, to be His own people, through whom He would reveal His nature.

In New Testament times the tradition continued: it was to the shepherds, not the wise men, that God sent the angels with the news of the Savior's birth. And it was a group of rough fishermen, not scholars, that Jesus picked for His closest friends, the ones to whom He would say, "Whoever has seen me has seen the Father" (John 14:9).

When Jesus contemplated the way God revealed Himself, He "rejoiced in the Holy Spirit and said, 'I offer you praise, O Father, Lord of heaven and earth, because what you have hidden from the learned and the clever you have revealed to the merest children' " (Luke 10:21).

Pope Paul VI recalled that moment in Jesus' life when he declared, "Spiritual exaltation bursts into our soul as we proclaim the humble and wise Dominican virgin a Doctor of the Church."[1] With those words, and in that spirit, he opened the official ceremonies in Saint Peter's Basilica. This concept lies at the very heart of the Church's understanding of Catherine and her writing: that she was a lowly, ignorant person who had received divine revelation, and as such she was part of an ancient and honored tradition in the Church.

Catherine saw herself in exactly that light. When she first sensed the call to leave seclusion and enter the world, she understood Jesus to say, "The pride of the so-called learned and wise has risen to such heights that I have resolved to humble them. I will therefore send unlearned men, full of divine wisdom, and women who will put to shame the learning that men think they have. I have resolved to send you also out into the world, and wheresoever you go I will be with you and never leave you, and I will guide you in all you must do."[2]

Paul VI talked about Catherine's "infused wisdom." He used the same term Pope Pius II used in 1461 when he wrote the bull of canonization that marked the Church's official recognition of Catherine as a saint. In so doing, he reaffirmed for the Church of the twentieth century the judgment made by the general chapter of the Dominicans when they met in Florence in 1374 to consider how Catherine acquired her knowledge. Catherine's doctrine was "infused wisdom" — that is, it came through divine revelation.

This, of course, was exactly what Catherine had always

said. She told Raymond of Capua that Jesus was her only Teacher. Raymond, in turn, made this point at great length in his official biography of her. Others of her friends, including Bartholomew Dominic, concur, declaring that even from the earliest days when she first began to form her circle of friends, she was always the teacher; the priests and Brothers and doctors were always the pupils. Even the professors from the University of Siena were her pupils.

Pope Paul VI gives this rather negative analysis of Catherine's theology, as we know it through her writings: "We shall certainly not find the apologetic vigor and the theological boldness which mark the works of the great lights of the ancient Church both in East and West. Nor can we expect the uncultivated virgin of Fontebranda to give us lofty speculations which belong to systematic theology and which made the Doctors of the scholastic middle ages immortal. It is true that her writings reflect the theology of the Angelic Doctor in a surprising degree, yet that theology appears there barren of any scientific clothing."[3]

But then he goes on to describe what the Church finds truly praiseworthy in her work: "What strikes us most about the saint is her infused wisdom. That is to say, lucid, profound and inebriating absorption of the divine truths and the mysteries of the faith contained in the Holy Books of the Old and New Testament."[4]

"Profound and inebriating absorption of the divine truths" filled Catherine's writing as well as her life. She received those deep revelations from God and she absorbed them into the very core of her being. And when she wrote about them, she wrote with astonishing accuracy and freshness. She was writing about her own very exciting experiences: about Jesus, the Person she loved, and about heaven, the homeland of her heart, the place where she yearned to be. Her accounts are personal and vivid, never dull, or distorted, or made to conform to previously learned ideas.

Pope Paul VI praises Catherine for her use of the gifts of wisdom, knowledge, and exhortation, all charismatic gifts mentioned by Saint Paul. "How many rays of superhuman wisdom," the pope ponders, "how many urgent calls to imitation of Christ in all the mysteries of His life and His suffering, how many efficacious teachings about the practice of the virtues proper to the various states in life, are scattered through the saint's works! Her letters are like so many sparks from a mysterious fire, lit in her ardent heart by Infinite Love, that is, the Holy Spirit."[5]

He also praises her as a mystic. "It seems to us that Catherine is the mystic of the Incarnate Word, above all of Jesus Crucified," he said. "She was one who exalted the redeeming power of the adorable Blood of the Son of God, shed on the wood of the cross in expanding love, for the salvation of all generations of mankind."[6]

But the Holy Father's greatest praise is for her attitude toward the Church and the papacy. Catherine loved the Church. She believed it to be a divine creation, perfect in structure, a channel for all of God's grace in our world, deserving of all loyalty, even worth dying for.

"What did she mean by renewal and reform of the Church?" Paul asked. "Certainly not the overthrow of its basic structures, rebellion against the pastors, a free rein for personal charisms, arbitrary innovations in worship and discipline, such as some would like in our day. On the contrary, she repeatedly affirms that beauty should be given back to the Spouse of Christ and it would be necessary to make reforms.

"She addressed her exhortations principally to sacred pastors, for she was disgusted and had holy scorn for the indolence of more than a few of them, and she fumed at their silence while the flock entrusted to them was lost and ruined."[7]

The reform Catherine wrote about was reform of the corrupt clergy, who needed purification to become worthy "ministers of the blood" of Christ; reform of the rebellious people who defied the pronouncements of their priests and their pope. Above all she wanted reform of all who were disloyal to the duly elected pope, to whom all the faithful owed absolute obedience.

"What deep respect then and passionate love did the saint not have for the Roman Pontiff!" Pope Paul VI exclaimed. "We Ourself, the least of the servants of God, personally owe Catherine immense gratitude today, certainly not because of the honor that might redound to our humble person, but because of the mystical apologia which she made for the apostolic office of Peter's successor. Who does not remember? In him she saw *il dolce Cristo in terra* — sweet Christ on earth. To him is due filial affection and obedience, because 'Whoever is disobedient to Christ on earth, who represents Christ in heaven, does not share in the fruit of the Blood of the Son of God.' "[8]

The Holy Father, in his proclamation, notes that Catherine not only wrote about reform of the Church but also lived for reform of the Church, and eventually offered her life as a willing sacrifice for the Church. As one of the proofs of Catherine's willingness to sacrifice for the Church, Paul VI cites her deathbed prayer: "O eternal God, receive the sacrifice of my life for the sake of this mystical body of the Church. I have nothing other to give but what Thou hast given me. Take my heart, therefore, and squeeze it out over the face of this spouse."[9]

The pope declared, "This message was typical of the new Doctor of the Church, Catherine of Siena. It enlightens and gives example to all who glory in belonging to the Church."[10]

The date chosen to confer the title of Doctor of the Church on this remarkable woman is deserving of some attention: October 4, 1970. It was the feast of Saint Francis, a reminder to all that there are two great saints from Tuscany, two great spiritual traditions, two great models for the faithful to follow.

The date was also, as Pope John Paul II has pointed out, five years after the close of the Second Vatican Council, and it is easy to find parallels between the documents of the council and the writings of the saint from Siena.

The six hundredth anniversary of Catherine's death was observed in 1980 and provided John Paul II with several opportunities to teach about her. His speeches and homilies are not official proclamations like the one Paul VI delivered in 1970, but they are of interest because they reveal the parts of Catherine's life and doctrine that he and modern Church scholars have found worthy of emulation. In an address delivered to eight thousand students in Rome in March of 1980, John Paul talked about the universal vocation to holiness, the idea that all Christians, no matter what their walk in life, are called to imitate Christ. He noted that this concept, which is spelled out by the Second Vatican Council in the fifth chapter of *Lumen Gentium*, was also spelled out by Catherine in her writings and in her life.

Quoting from *Lumen Gentium* John Paul said, "It is clear that all Christians in any state or walk of life are called to the fullness of Christian life and to the perfection of love. . . . The Lord Jesus, divine teacher and model of all perfection, preached holiness of life (of which He is the author and maker) to each and every one of His disciples without distinction. . . ."[11]

The pontiff went on: "These concepts had been clearly expressed six hundred years earlier by Catherine of Siena, the centenary of whose death, or rather, of her entrance into 'lasting life,' as she called eternal life, occurs at this time. The basic subject of all her teaching consists precisely in indicating to everyone the duty of responding to the divine call. In all her writings, *The Dialogue*, the letters, the prayers, this fundamental element of her apostolate always recurs."[12]

Pope John Paul II quoted a man named Aldo Manuzio, who prepared Catherine's letters for publication in the year

1500 and was so moved by them that he wrote to a friend, "He who reads these letters, cannot but reform completely, that is, become holy: because these letters are like powerful preachers, who oblige people to do what they advise."[13]

The Holy Father quoted from *The Dialogue*, too, where the call to holiness is explained with uncompromising clarity: ". . . no one can draw back saying, 'I have my profession, I have children, or other encumbrances of the world; for this reason I draw back and do not follow this way.' They cannot say so because I already told you that every state was agreeable and acceptable to me (God), provided it was carried out with a good and holy will. Nor can it be objected that holiness is too difficult to reach. Holiness, in fact, is an easy thing, but nothing is so easy and so delightful as love. And what I ask of you is nothing but love and delight in me and your neighbor."[14]

For Catherine, of course, holiness was not just something to write about, it was her very life. The Holy Father acknowledged that, saying that she "spent the short thirty-three years of her earthly existence in continual spiritual ascent."[15]

In his next homily on Saint Catherine, in April of 1980, John Paul talked mostly about that life. "She is a marvelous woman," he declared, "who in that second half of the fourteenth century shows in herself what a human creature, and — I stress — a woman, the daughter of humble dyers, was made capable of, when she can listen to the voice of the one Pastor and Teacher, and nourish herself at the table of the divine Bridegroom, to whom, as a 'wise virgin,' she has generously consecrated her life. We have here a masterpiece of grace, renewing and raising the creature to the perfection of holiness, which is also the full realization of the fundamental values of humanity."[16]

In that same homily, he paid tribute to Catherine's understanding of Scripture. The Gospel of the day was the parable of the wise and foolish virgins, and the pope took the occasion to quote from a letter Catherine had written to a young niece about what the parable meant. But mostly on that day he talked about Catherine's life, the richness of her humanity, which was perfected by God's grace, her great natural talents made even greater because she united her will with that of Jesus.

Later that year John Paul II published an apostolic letter on the sixth centenary of Catherine's death. In it, again, he dwelt more on her life than on her writings. He continued the theme Paul VI used ten years earlier, marveling at God's way of using unlikely people to be His instruments on earth. He talked about her great spiritual development, her loyalty to the Church, and her way of life among her followers. He also mentioned her stigmata, probably the only time either he or his predecessor acknowledged any miraculous happening in Catherine's life.

In the apostolic letter, the Holy Father makes passing reference to Catherine's theology. He calls her prayers "bold but absolutely orthodox"[17] and says *The Dialogue* anticipates the writing of Saint John of the Cross. He makes special note of the way she uses the image of the bridge to explain how Jesus is the means of our salvation. He has unreserved praise for her Christology as she develops that image which is the very heart of *The Dialogue*.

In the letter, John Paul draws another parallel between Catherine's theology and the documents of Vatican II. The council taught that love of neighbor was inseparable from love of God. In an era when many Christians thought more about their relationship with God than their relationship with other people, Catherine taught that love of God had no meaning without love of neighbor, that love of God could not be expressed except through love of neighbor, and that our salvation depends on our relationships with our neighbors.

Finally in September, 1980, Pope John Paul II delivered a major homily in Siena in which he returned to that favorite theme: the greatness of human life when it is lived with grace.

"Let us not forget the great works of God!" he cried, opening the sermon. He continued, saying that Catherine herself was a marvelous work of God. "All that she was, all that she did in the course of her life of barely thirty-three years, was a marvelous work of God himself. It was a work of the Holy Spirit, to whom the wise virgin was submissive and obedient, resembling that sublime woman who remains for us a model beyond reach: the mother of the Savior."[18]

He praised her teachings on mystic prayer, and on the exaltation of the cross. He praised her for her work as a peacemaker between Florence and the Holy See, and for her work to bring the papal court back to Rome. But most of all, he praised that enormous miracle — the presence of God in her life, the presence of God in human life.

"We come to Siena today to recall, after six hundred years, that particular work of God that had its beginning here: Catherine of Siena. We come not only to remember her in this city, but also to bless God for her and through her: to give thanks to God for the work that He wanted to accomplish in her and through her within the history of the Church and the history of Italy. After six centuries, this work is still alive, and it still has its particular eloquence. Catherine of Siena lives in God that life which was first infused into her through Baptism. . . . And this life of hers in God, in the tabernacle of the Most Blessed Trinity, reconfirms in a definitive way the truth of the words once uttered by Saint Irenaeus, a Father of the Church in the second century: 'the glory of God is living man.' "[19]

These two modern popes, when they have spoken and written about this remarkable woman who was both an illiterate and a Doctor of the Church, have often pointed out that the faithful can learn as much from her life as from her writings. The aspect of her life mentioned most often as worthy of attention is her voluntary suffering for the sake of the Church. Other aspects of her life, underscored by the popes as worthy of study and emulation, include the care of the poor and the sick, her personal purity, and her faithfulness to prayer.

It is significant that the popes do not mention Catherine's eating pattern, making only passing reference to her very severe penances and self-mortification. These extreme ascetic practices were a central part of the spirituality of Catherine's time. As we have seen, they were followed by many holy people. For that reason, such practices do not need to be condemned today. But neither are they held up by our popes as practices that the faithful should follow.

13

Some of Catherine's Ideas

Saint Catherine was a great teacher. She loved to talk about God and heaven and the revelations she received. She loved to direct people's lives, telling them what they needed to do and how and why. In her letters we can see this drive to enlighten and guide. As Pope Paul VI said, "Her letters are like so many sparks from a mysterious fire, lit in her ardent heart by Infinite Love, that is, the Holy Spirit." Her conversations with friends had that same fire, that same burning desire to help people grow closer to God.

During the last weeks and months of her life, as she suffered her long, last agony, she continued to teach and exhort and guide. Her last words, as recorded by her loyal friends, go on for pages and pages with advice for every one of her followers. She had lost control of her body, and could not speak above a whisper, but what little energy was left, she spent on teaching.

She had already prepared for the time when she would not be with them. She had written her *Book*, as she called it, the classic now known as *The Dialogue*. It is a series of teachings in the form of conversations between God and a soul. In them, God teaches the soul how to pray, how to love more perfectly, how to follow the Way who is Jesus. The themes of this work were central to Catherine's life and her teaching. Catherine wanted these truths written down so her followers would have them even when she was not alive to teach them.

Recognizing Saint Catherine's desire to share what she received with all of her followers, we include in this chapter some of the truths she taught most often.

The Cell of Self-Knowledge • When Catherine was an adolescent, struggling against her parents' prohibition against prayer, she built a cell within herself where she could always pray. This cell saved her sanity during those difficult years and determined the direction of her spirituality for the rest of her days.

She had discovered one of the basic principles of contemplative prayer. Other great contemplatives have called this interior space by other names. Catherine called it the "cell of self-knowledge," and she considered it essential to spiritual progress.

"Make two homes for thyself, my daughter," she wrote to Alessia Saracini, "one actual home in thy cell . . . and another spiritual home, which thou art to carry with thee always — the cell of true self-knowledge where thou shalt find within thyself knowledge of the goodness of God."[1]

This cell is the starting place for all spiritual growth because within it the soul finds knowledge of God and knowledge of herself.* Knowledge of God leads the soul to love God, to seek Him, to obey Him. Knowledge of self leads the soul to be humble, to know her own sin and to hate it. Without knowledge of God and His infinite love, the soul would despair at her own sinfulness. Without knowledge of her own sin, the

---

*In referring to the soul in *The Dialogue*, Catherine used the feminine instead of the neuter gender: "she" instead of "it," and so on; we will follow Catherine's technique throughout this chapter whenever we refer to the soul.

soul might become proud because she receives so much love from God.

The soul who has knowledge of both herself and God can embark on the great spiritual journey, growing in imitation of God and in time becoming "one thing with God."

God's Love for Humans • "I loved you before you came into being," God tells the soul in *The Dialogue*, "and in my unspeakable love for you I willed to create you anew in grace. So I washed you and made you a new creation in the blood that my only-begotten Son poured out with such burning love."[2]

In a restatement of a familiar line from Holy Scripture, God tells the soul, "The eye cannot see, nor the tongue tell, nor can the heart imagine how many paths and methods I have, solely for love and to lead them back to grace so that my truth may be realized in them."[3]

The love of God that Catherine experienced led her to say that God was crazy with love for us. She did not think this love was justified. She saw many reasons why God should not love us, many sins that could drive Him away. But experience taught her that sin never stopped God's love. In spite of sin God reaches out to us again and again, even sending His Son to us. Such love is not rational. Catherine could only describe it as "insanity."

The Beauty of Human Nature • Much of Catherine's writing is concerned with sin and how it offends God. The underlying premise, seldom stated but always implied, is that without the devastation brought on by sin, humans are beautiful creatures. The gift of "illumination," which Catherine received after she prayed faithfully for Palmerina, revealed both the beauty of souls and the ugliness of sin. (As you may recall, Palmerina was the jealous Mantellata who spread vicious lies about Catherine, but repented just before she died.) The beauty Catherine saw in souls was overwhelming and gave her reason to work and pray all her life for the salvation of souls.

In the Prologue to *The Dialogue* she tells of a time when God revealed this beauty to her. "Open your mind's eye and look within me, and you will see the dignity and beauty of my reasoning creature," He told her. "But beyond the beauty I have given the soul by creating her in my image and likeness, look at those who are clothed in the wedding garment of charity, adorned with many true virtues: they are united with me through love."[4] The souls who unite themselves with Jesus attain the highest possible level of beauty. They drown their own self-wills; conforming themselves completely to the will of Christ, they become another Christ.

This view of humanity forms the very foundation of Catherine's work. Man is intrinsically beautiful, created in God's image; he is capable, by living with much love, of resembling Jesus, even being another Jesus. Sin distorts and destroys human beauty.

Self-Will • Drowning, crushing, denying her self-will and obeying instead the will of Jesus, was one of the great goals of Catherine's life. She was influenced here by a line from John's Gospel in which Jesus says, "Anyone who loves me will be true to my word, and my Father will love him; we will come to him and make our dwelling place with him" (John 14:22). That is the translation the Church uses today, but the translation Catherine knew had quite a different meaning. It might be rendered in English as, "If you love me and keep my word, I will show myself to you, and you will be one thing with me and I with you."

Catherine was willing to do anything to become "one thing with Jesus." All of her fasting and self-denial had this goal in mind. She wanted to kill her own selfish will so she could more perfectly obey the will of Jesus.

Fasting and Penance • Catherine was ruthless concerning her own life and with her own body. But she did not preach what she herself practiced.

She developed her own program of austerities when she was young and enthusiastic. She loved Jesus with the passion of an adolescent and thought she could prove that love through suffering. The program she worked out, and lived out, was immature and immoderate.

As she matured, she began to see suffering in a different light, as a tool to control the will, not a goal to be sought for its own sake. Severe fasting, self-punishment, and suffering were still considered signs of holiness by most of her contemporaries, but Catherine did not recommend them to others. She recommended moderation in everything except love for God.

Writing to a housewife in Florence, Monna Agnese, she told her not to fast except on the days specified by the Church, and only when she felt able.

Writing to Sister Daniella of Orvieta, a contemplative who had become sick through severe fasting and penances, she warned against losing perspective and seeing penance as a goal in itself. "Perfection does not consist in macerating or killing the body, but in killing our perverse self-will," she said. "If the flesh being too strong, kicks against the spirit, penance takes the rod of discipline, and fast, and the saying of many beads, and nightly vigils, and places burdens enough on the flesh, that it may be subdued. But if the body is weak, fallen into illness, the rule of discretion does not approve of such method. I have already seen many penitents who have been neither patient or obedient because they studied to kill their bodies, not their wills."[5]

Suffering • The aspect of Jesus' life that riveted Saint Catherine's attention was not His teaching or His healing, not His birth or His resurrection, but His suffering. The image of Christ crucified was always before her. In order to grow more like Him, she inflicted suffering upon herself as a daily routine, gratefully accepting all pain, both physical and mental, that came into her life.

This suffering-centered spirituality may seem foreign to today's believers, who live at a time when the Church emphasizes wholeness and wholesomeness as essential parts of holiness, and who constantly hear the popular culture advising people to shun pain and seek instant gratification. But in Catherine's day most Christians accepted suffering as an important element in their spiritual journey. From the time of Saint Anthony and the other desert Fathers until the late Middle Ages, most people seeking a close relationship with God used the tools of prayer, fasting, and suffering to achieve their goal.

Suffering filled Catherine's life and her teachings. "No one born into this life passes through it without suffering of body or spirit," Eternal Truth declares in *The Dialogue*. "My servants may suffer physically, but their spirit is free. In other words, suffering does not weary them, because their will is in tune with mine. It is the will that causes the deeper pain. Those I have described to you, who taste already in this life the pledge of hell, suffer spiritually as well as physically, while my servants taste the pledge of eternal life."[6]

Suffering Offered for the Reparation of Sins ● Contemplating the crucified Christ as she did so often, Catherine was overwhelmed by the way sin offends God. She wanted to undo that offense, to make reparation to God. She wanted to relieve God's suffering. She wanted to give God all the suffering she could cram into her life as a loving gift, so He would suffer less.

It is no simple thing for the soul, a finite creature, to make reparation to her infinite Creator. In *The Dialogue* she struggled to understand and to explain the great mystery of suffering and reparation.

"Do you know, my daughter," Truth asks the soul, "that all the suffering the soul bears or can bear in this life are not enough to punish one smallest sin? For an offense against me, infinite Good, demands infinite satisfaction. . . . Finite works are not enough either to punish or to atone unless they are seasoned with loving charity. . . . In this life, guilt is not atoned for by any suffering simply as suffering, but rather by suffering borne with desire, love, and contrition of heart."[7]

Truth expands on this theme of finite works becoming infinitely worthy: "I want works of penance and other bodily practices to be undertaken as [a] means, not as your chief goal. By making them your chief goal you would be giving me a finite thing — like a word that comes out of the mouth and then ceases to exist — unless indeed that word comes out of the soul's love, which conceives virtue and brings it to birth in truth. I mean that finite works — which I have likened to words — must be joined with loving charity. Such works . . . would please me."[8]

Suffering Seen as God's Correction • The major reason for suffering, as Catherine understood it, was for the punishment of sins. But this was by no means the only reason for suffering. "I want you to know," says Eternal Truth, "that not all sufferings given in this life are given for punishment, but rather for correction, to chastise the child who offends."[9]

This became an important principle of Catherine's life. She applied it especially to mental suffering that came her way. When she was publicly criticized and misunderstood, her followers would take great offense and want her to defend herself, to speak out against the critics and prove them wrong. But Catherine would accept the criticism meekly, taking it to heart, examining it to see what she could learn from it, how she could change to make herself more pleasing to God. Her assumption always was that the real source of the criticism was not of human but divine origin: it was God trying again to correct and perfect the daughter He loved.

The Bridge • The longest and most important section of *The Dialogue* is called "The Bridge." God uses this image to explain to the soul His plan for salvation, which is Jesus. With His feet planted in the clay of the earth, and His head reaching the heavens, Jesus is the bridge that unites us with our Creator.

Sin, the disobedience of Adam and Eve, created a rushing turbulent river where Satan reigns and tries to lure mankind. But God did not want His beautiful creatures to suffer and drown in those waters, so He sent His Son to be a bridge for mankind, restoring with His truth and His obedience the path destroyed by the lies of Satan and the sin of Adam and Eve. By uniting His divinity with our humanity, Jesus became the bridge that stretches from earth to heaven.

The bridge has three stairs, representing the three spiritual stages the faithful must pass through to attain eternal life.

The first stair is the feet of Christ, nailed to the wood of the cross. Souls who climb this stair are dominated by their emotions, which carry the soul as the feet carry the body. They are especially dominated by fear, fear of pain. Many become discouraged on the first stair and turn back because of fear.

But if the souls persevere, they arrive at the second stair, the wound in the side of Christ, where they see God's love for them and are filled with love. They turn away from their sins, and their transformation begins.

The third stair is the mouth of Christ, where the soul tastes peace and rests from her battle over sin. This stair can be reached only by those who have climbed the other two — who have battled their sins and been filled with Christ's love. The floodwaters never reach them here.

From the third stair the soul can reach the fourth stair, which is heaven. Souls who reach that stair have attained perfect love and obedience. They move freely in and out of heaven, experiencing the bliss themselves and helping others along the path.

Other aspects of salvation are explained in the bridge image: the bridge has walls of mercy and likewise a roof of mercy so the faithful can walk upon the bridge without fear of being caught in the rain of divine justice. God's mercy came to earth at the incarnation, saving man from the punishment God's justice would have imposed.

The faithful who travel the bridge walk in the light of truth and are refreshed at the hostelry of the Church, where the Bread of Life and the Blood are served by God's ministers so no one has to grow faint along the way.

On the bridge there is a gate, the gate of truth: our Lord and Savior, Jesus. It is a very narrow gate, but it is the only way to enter heaven.

The bridge is raised very high. Jesus said, "I — once I am lifted up from Earth — will draw all men to myself" (John 12:32). Through the bridge Jesus draws all mankind, and all human gifts, so they can be put at the service of His Father in heaven.

The bridge has stairs so souls can travel from slavish fear to perfect love in steps that they can handle.

The souls who travel along the bridge are souls who are earnestly seeking God. They have renounced sin and are struggling toward perfection. Catherine is fascinated by them and their struggle. She cares about every detail of the dangers and hardships they face; she rejoices at each grace that the Father of mercy sends them. When she writes about these souls, of course, she is writing about lives she knows, her own struggles and graces, and those of her close friends. When she records the exhortations and admonishments of God, she is giving her friends and followers the best advice she can.

The Turbulent Waters of Sin and Desire • Below the bridge is the raging torrent where Satan lives. He lures souls by lying to them about the pleasures of sin, taking advantage of their self-love, their desire for pleasure, and their fear of pain.

The souls who submerge themselves fully in the river of sin and desire lose control of their lives. There is no rock on which to stand, only the raging waters of temptation. There is no restraining the water and no possibility of reaching solid ground again. The souls live out their days in terrible fear and darkness, without the light of truth, buffeted about by waves of desire and temptation, until, at last, they drown.

Not all souls are fooled by Satan's hook. Some try the waters cautiously, see the sin, and turn away from it in time and try the bridge instead. Others can tell just by looking that they would prefer the bridge to the tumult of the stream.

The First Step — Slavish Fear • Most souls seek God and His ways because they are afraid of sin. They have seen the consequences of sin, the pain and suffering, and they turn away in fear and try to find God instead. They are the people on the first stair. They are trying to strip themselves of sin because they fear the consequences. Many of these fearful souls move along sluggishly, get discouraged, and turn back. Others persevere for a time, but then the winds of prosperity blow, or adversity comes, and they turn back. No one stays still on the path. Either the soul moves toward God and perfect love, or falls back into worldly concerns and temptations. Fear is useful as a motive to get the soul onto the bridge, but fear alone cannot sustain her through the whole journey. In order to persevere on the path the soul must move beyond slavish fear and acquire love of virtue. She gets help for this at the second stair.

The Second Step — Imperfect Love • The soul who reaches the second stair gazes into the wound in the side of Christ. She sees His love, feels His love, and begins to love with His love. Fear is no longer her only motive for doing good; she has begun to love virtue for its own sake.

The second stair is a time of transition and transformation, and most people spend their lives there. Souls on the first stair offer God the love and obedience of slaves who act out of fear. Souls on the second stair offer Him the love of faithful servants or friends who love with imperfect or selfish love. They love for their own sake; they seek their own pleasure.

They pray because they experience the comfort of God's presence in prayer. Prayer, for them, is a pleasurable, sensual experience. If God withdraws from them the awareness of His presence, many of them stop praying. God does withdraw this awareness, from time to time, because He wants to train His faithful ones to seek Him rather than mere comfort.

Those on the second stair care too much about created things: people and possessions. All things created are good, but none is as good as the Creator, and none should be desired more than the Creator.

Mothers are especially vulnerable to disordered selfish love. They love their children without thinking of them as God's children first. They seek their own pleasure and comfort from their children. They want the pleasure of their children's company; they want the comfort of being proud of the way their children succeed. They should be seeking God's will for their children and encouraging their children to seek it.

The greatest danger to the souls whose love is imperfect is fear of suffering. They love their own bodies and their own feelings too much; they fear anything that might hurt them. They are ruled by "servile fear." They are cowards and not "manly men." Catherine exhorted everyone, male and female alike, to act like "manly men."

Pope Gregory XI was a man who struggled with fear of suffering. He was afraid of offending his family and advisers, afraid of how he would suffer if he hurt them, so he postponed the return to Rome. That servile fear kept him from uniting his will with God's. With Catherine's help, of course, he was able to overcome that fear and follow what he believed was God's will.

It is not easy for the soul to make the complete transition from selfish love to perfect love. God provides many means of grace to help her along the way, one of which is the cell of self-knowledge.

Catherine cites Saint Peter as a man who progressed from imperfect to perfect love of God, by means of the cell of self-knowledge. At first Peter followed Jesus because he enjoyed His company. When Jesus said that He had to go up to Jerusalem and be killed, Peter protested vehemently. He did not want to lose the comfort of Christ's presence. He did not know or accept God's will for Jesus; he just wanted Jesus with him. In the Garden of Gethsemane when Jesus asked him to stay awake, he chose the pleasure of sleep instead. Later he acted out of fear and not loyalty, first by running away from the soldiers, then by three times denying that he knew Jesus.

But, of course, Peter's story does not end with his denials. He repented of those denials, fought against his fears, and sought Jesus again. Obeying Christ's instructions then, after He ascended, Peter went with the others to the upper room to pray until the Holy Spirit came. Catherine believed that the experience the Apostles had in the upper room was comparable to the experience she had in her cell of self-knowledge. He emerged from the upper room a transformed person. He knew God. His love had been transformed from selfish to perfect. He went out to live a life of courageous service according to God's will.

The Third Step — Perfect Love ● The third stair of the bridge is the mouth of Christ, where the soul tastes peace and finds rest. She has survived all the trials and dangers of the second stair. She has found the cell of self-knowledge and been transformed there. She has let go of "the hell of self-will" and conformed her will to God's. She loves now with perfect love and experiences eternal life.

In this state, God tells the soul, "they receive supernatural light, and in that light they love me. For love follows upon understanding. The more they know, the more they love,

171

and the more they love, the more they know. Thus each nourishes the other. By this light they reach that eternal vision of me in which they see and taste me in truth when soul is separated from body. . . . This is that superb state in which the soul even while still mortal shares the enjoyment of the immortals."[10]

The soul who reaches this blissful state, tasting the joys of heaven, does not cling to it, but freely relinquishes it to work for the honor and glory of God and the salvation of souls. Saint Paul had this experience, and says in his letter to the Philippians that he does not know which he prefers: to stay alive for the sake of the souls he can save, or die and be united with Christ. The Apostles had a similar experience at Pentecost, Catherine believed. And, of course, she had many experiences of union with God, the greatest of which was probably her mystic betrothal to Jesus, which was followed almost immediately by her public ministry.

Vocal Prayer and Mental Prayer ● "Perfect prayer," God says in *The Dialogue*, "is achieved not with many words but with loving desire, when the soul rises up to me with knowledge of herself, each movement seasoned by the other. In this way she will have vocal and mental prayer at the same time, for the two stand together like the active life and the contemplative life."[11]

According to *The Dialogue* the soul does not start out, of course, with perfect prayer. She should start with vocal prayer, reading or reciting a number of psalms, or Our Fathers, at an appointed hour each day. She should not rush through this vocal prayer caring only about the number of prayers she says. Neither should she concentrate on the words of the vocal prayer to the exclusion of all else.

"While she says the words," God recommends, "she should make an effort to concentrate on my love, pondering at the same time her own sins and the blood of my only-begotten Son. There she will find the expansiveness of my charity and forgiveness for her sins. Thus self-knowledge and the consideration of her sins ought to bring her to know my goodness to her and make her continue her exercise in true humility."

The soul should not think about her sins individually "lest her mind be contaminated by the memory." But rather she should think about her sins generally, at the same time calling to mind the blood of Christ and the greatness of God's mercy.

As the soul prays in this way, God says, "I may visit her spirit in one way or another, sometimes with a flash of self-knowledge and contrition for her sinfulness, sometimes in the greatness of my love setting before her mind the presence of my Truth in different ways, depending on my pleasure or her longings." When the soul senses her spirit ready for such a visitation, she should abandon her vocal prayer in favor of the mental prayer. Only a very foolish person would shut out such a visit to persist in vocal prayer. But when the visit is over, if there is time, the soul may return to her vocal prayer, as she wishes.

The soul who perseveres with her vocal prayer, abandoning it for mental prayer as she senses God's will to be with her, will advance step by step toward perfect prayer. "She will experience prayer in truth," God says, "and that food which is the body and blood of my only-begotten Son. . . . Some souls communicate in the body and blood of Christ actually, even though not sacramentally, when they communicate in loving charity, which they enjoy in holy prayer, in proportion to their desire."

Love of Neighbor • There are only two reasons to abandon prayer. One is obedience, if a superior or director demands it. The other is to serve the needs of a neighbor.

A soul cannot grow in prayer or love if she refuses to help her neighbor in need, on the pretext that such help will interfere with her prayer or disturb her spiritual peace. A person who says such things is deluded and will not find God in prayer. On the other hand, the person who abandons prayer because a neighbor has a need will find God in the loving service rendered to the neighbor.

The goal of prayer is to bring the soul to greater love of God and therefore to greater love of neighbor. The soul who reaches the stage of perfect love, and is united with God, leaves that bliss to serve her neighbor, because she loves her neighbor as God does.

Love for God is expressed through service to neighbor. God does not need our service, but His creatures do.

Mystical Union with God and the Ecstatic State • Catherine spent many hours rapt in prayer — that is, in an ecstatic state. A significant portion of her adult life was spent this way. Her friends reported that at these times her body became rigid. Raymond of Capua said that it would be easier to break her bones than to loosen her grip if she was holding something when she was in a state of rapture. Lapa once tried to straighten her up and nearly broke her neck. Catherine ached for days afterward. Her friends consistently reported that when she was rapt, she did not respond to sights or sounds or touch in any way. She did speak, however. She often prayed aloud and dictated major portions of *The Dialogue* when in the rapt state.

In that work, God gives this explanation of the ecstatic state: "The soul does not really leave the body (this happens only in death), but her powers and emotions are united with me in love. Therefore the memory finds itself filled with nothing but me. The understanding is lifted up as it gazes into my Truth. The will, which always follows the understanding, loves and unites itself with what the eye of understanding sees. When these powers are gathered and united all together and immersed and set afire in me, the body loses its feeling. For the eye sees without seeing; the ear hears without hearing; the tongue speaks without speaking (except that sometimes, because of the heart's fullness, I will let the tongue speak for the unburdening of the heart and for the glory and praise of my name, so that it speaks without speaking); . . ."[12]

Catherine gave several different kinds of reports about what happened while she was in this state. Sometimes she described heaven and what was going on, the celebration of a saint's feast day, for instance. She could give details about who was there and what they said and did. Sometimes she would return with instructions for her companions, or with a new way to understand a familiar truth. There were other times when she could not describe the experience. It was so different from normal human experience that there were no words to describe it in human language.

One day while she was rapt in this way she began to repeat the phrase "I have seen the secret things of God." When she woke, Raymond of Capua asked why she said that, and what she had seen. But she could not explain anything to him. "On this occasion I am so conscious of how inadequate human words are to express what I saw. I should feel as if I were only belittling God, and profaning Him, by any words I could say."[13]

On another occasion Catherine said she could feel her soul melt into the love of God. On still another occasion, when she received Holy Communion, she felt her soul enter into God and God enter into her soul, in somewhat the same way that a fish is in the water and the water is in a fish, for lack of a better way to explain it.

The Blood of Christ • Catherine, who spent days and years of her life praying before the crucifix, found tremendous meaning in the blood of Christ. By the blood we have been redeemed, she taught; by the blood our sins are forgiven. The body of Christ feeds and sustains us; the blood of Christ cleanses us of our sins. The blood of Christ flows through the Church to all

175

the world. The priests and bishops are ministers of the blood of Christ.

"All the Church's sacraments derive their value and life-giving power from His blood,"[14] she wrote in *The Dialogue*. And again, in that book, God explains confession to the soul, saying, "So my divine charity had to leave them an ongoing baptism of blood accessible by heartfelt contrition and a holy confession as soon as they can confess to my ministers who hold the key to the blood. This blood the priest pours over the soul in absolution."[15]

In all of these references, the blood of Christ is mentioned in connection with redemption and forgiveness. In Catherine's life the blood was also associated with nourishment. Raymond of Capua recounts an experience she had one day when she was not allowed to receive Holy Communion, and sat in the back of the church hungering. "Nor did our Savior refuse her desire," he wrote. "He appeared to her, as He now was long accustomed to do, and pressed her mouth to the wound in His side, inviting her to slake her thirst to the full with His body and blood. She did not hesitate: eagerly she drank of the floods of life which flowed from the fountain of His sacred breast. As she drank, her soul was swept by rapture of such delight that she felt she was about to die of very love. But when her confessor later questioned her as to what exactly it was that she had experienced at that moment, she could only reply that it was a thing which could not be expressed in words."[16]

As you will recall, Catherine's very last thoughts and prayers in this life were about the blood of Christ. She asked God to show her mercy, not because she deserved it, but because of the merits of the blood of Jesus. "Blood, blood, blood," she cried, spending her very last energy on the words. Then she whispered, "Father, into Thy hands I commend my spirit." And so she died, as she had lived, contemplating the blood of her Savior.

14

Saint Catherine: Myth or Model?

Catherine of Siena lived long ago and far away, in a world that was very different from ours. Many aspects of that world are hard for us to grasp: the political power of the popes, the decadence of the papal court in Avignon, the continual unrest and civil disorder of the great cities of Lombardy and Tuscany, the use of blood feuds to settle differences, to mention just a few.

Catherine herself is not easy for us to understand, with her suffering-centered spirituality, her flowery language, her retinue of devoted followers, her fasting, her miracles.

It is tempting to dismiss her story as a pious legend, a tale told by people who loved Catherine and miracles more than they loved truth. It is hard to believe what Raymond of Capua and the others said about her because they are so openly prejudiced in her favor, and because the story they tell is so foreign to our experience. But the testimony of Rudolph Bell, discussed in Chapter 11, sheds new light on the writings of Blessed Raymond and Saint Catherine's other friends, and gives us reason to think they may contain more fact than fiction.

Bell says that Catherine's friends describe her fasting and

her attitude toward food so accurately that the disease of anorexia can be detected from their writings. The comments about eating, fasting, and suffering — which they attribute to her — are strikingly similar to the comments made by today's anorectics. If these writers were accurate describing their dear friend's eating habits, there is a good chance that they were accurate about the rest of Catherine's life. The Catherine they present to us may not be a sentimental exaggeration, too fantastic to be true. She may be a real holy woman, different from us and the people we know, but still real.

Catherine is not merely a myth, then; but is she therefore a model for today's Christians? Catherine was very different from us. Her culture was different from ours, and so were her natural and spiritual gifts. But these very differences make her precious to us because they can give us a new perspective on our own lives and times.

Fasting • One of the most obvious differences between Catherine and most of today's faithful is in the way we approach fasting. For her, fasting was a tool used to discipline her selfish will. She wanted her will to be weak so Christ's will could be strong in her life. She wanted to kill her self-will, her selfish "self," so Christ could reign. Her goal was to please God, to obey God, and she never lost sight of that goal. In the spirit of Saint Paul, she was like an athlete who ran the race to win. She trained her mind and body to achieve her goal. Every form of fasting, every act of self-denial, was part of her training. She approached fasting with tremendous enthusiasm, perhaps too much enthusiasm. She rejoiced in every opportunity she found to deny her body's cravings.

The contrast with our own age could not be sharper. Self-denial is not a source of joy to many of us. Self-fulfillment is what we seek, we who are part of the "me" generation, or who helped to produce that generation. We talk about doing our own thing, and our most popular singers declare with pride,

"I did it my way." Fasting, for most of us, has become a minor inconvenience in our lives, a matter of remembering which days of Lent we need to find a substitute for meat in our diets.

Most of us grew up thinking of fasting as simply not eating meat on Fridays, and postponing breakfast until after Mass Sunday morning. We were happy to give up even those small fasts after the Second Vatican Council, when our bishops suggested that we might find more meaningful forms of penance.

Fasting has a long and honored history in the Roman Catholic Church, in Judaism, and in many of the Eastern religions as well. Fasting has been used not only to help people get in touch with God but also to help them discipline their appetites. Fasting is one of the most powerful spiritual tools available to us, yet few Catholics understand or practice it any more.

We do not fast. We avoid self-denial. How interested are we really in doing God's will? We want God's will, of course, especially if it is the same as ours. We want to want God's will. We pray the Our Father hoping that the words will transform us into people who want God's will done on earth as it is in heaven. We may even give God permission to work that transformation in us. But few of us actively seek to know God's will and obey it with anything like the determination Catherine brought to the task.

Suffering • Catherine's attitude toward suffering offers another dramatic contrast with the attitude that prevails today. She not only accepted the suffering that came her way, but actively sought additional suffering. She offered a variety of reasons for this. Suffering can atone for sin. It can be a pleasing offering to God. It lets the soul imitate Christ. It disciplines the body. Catherine saw suffering as good for the soul and pleasing to God.

Our society, on the other hand, sees suffering as something to avoid. We do not seek it out, and if it comes our way we do not welcome it. We use chemicals to subdue both physical and emotional pain we cannot otherwise avoid.

We seek pleasure the way Catherine sought suffering. Instant gratification is a staple of our society. Advertisers spend billions each year convincing us that we want any number of luxuries we do not need. Young people grow up unable to distinguish between their needs and their wants, and believing they have a right to both.

Many responsible people within the Church speak out against our American pursuit of luxury, especially since it contrasts so vividly with the hunger and disease of Third World countries and the plight of the poor at home. But few would recommend that the faithful pursue suffering the way Catherine did. Her approach to suffering was a product of her time and culture. It would not fit naturally into ours.

Yet suffering remains a real part of our lives, a mystery that troubles and fascinates us. We could learn a lot from Catherine's writings on suffering, even though we might not choose to imitate her actions.

There was one surprising fruit of suffering in her life that we should not overlook: when she began to impose suffering on herself in earnest, she became filled with zeal for the salvation of souls. There seemed to be a deep connection between the two. As she suffered, and contemplated Christ's suffering, she seemed to understand His love for souls, and to feel that love herself. That love for souls, that zeal for the salvation of souls, was a major motivation for Catherine and many of the great saints of the Church. It is seldom mentioned in the Church today.

Contemplating the Crucifixion • Closely associated with Catherine's ideas on suffering is her devotion to Christ crucified. "The Mystic of Jesus Crucified," Pope Paul VI called her. Her spirituality was based on the contemplation of the crucifix, and she came to know God's love through that contemplation.

Many spiritual directors in the Church nowadays would caution against focusing on the crucifixion to the exclusion of the other great events in Christ's life, especially the resurrection and ascension. We who can read, and have Bibles easily available to us, are encouraged and expected to contemplate all of Christ's life and teaching. For us to focus our attention on one event would be a distortion. For Catherine it was a necessity. She could not read, so she contemplated the crucifix. Through the crucifix she learned so much that she has been named a Doctor of the Church. Her exclusivity might not be a good model for us, but her willingness to learn about Jesus with the tools available to her is both model and inspiration.

A Life of Enormous Love • Catherine's fasting and suffering fascinate us perhaps because they are so very different from our own lives, but they were not the dominant forces in her life. The dominant force in her life was love. And in this area we can think of her as a model without any reservations.

Catherine first encountered God's love when she was six, when Jesus appeared to her in a vision, communicating to her in a way she understood that He loved her and that He wanted her to receive His love. It seems an awesome thing that a young child would receive such a vision, that Jesus would deign to make such an appearance. But the essential meaning of the vision, that very personal communication of God's love, has been received by other children. Many young children, especially those who have grown up hearing about God's love, have a personal experience of that love during their preschool years.

It is not unusual for a first-grader to say that he knows God loves him because of some incident in his life. "I know God loves me because my mother and father do," a six-year-old might assert, and be absolutely sure of his ground. Or "I know God loves me because he let my daddy live," a child might say, remembering how God answered his prayer. To an adult observer the first-grader's incident may not seem impressive, but to the child the incident is all he needs. God has communicated to him in a way he understands.

The account we have of Catherine's first great vision seems much more complete and impressive than anything a young child might experience; but, of course, that account was not the description of a young child. It was described to Raymond of Capua when she was an adult, using adult language, and remembering both the vision and many happy years of meditating on the vision.

Catherine's initial experience may not have been radically different from the experience of other young children, but her response to that experience was. She cherished the message of love she received, keeping its memory fresh through her play and prayer. She believed the message and let it become the very foundation of her life. She accepted the message and opened the very depths of her being to the love that it promised. Other children might forget the message and go on to other things in life. Catherine clung to the message, basking in the love of God it promised for the rest of her life.

She lived a life of enormous love. "Great Heart" we could call her because her capacity for love was so vast. Few people have ever received as much love, from God and man, or returned love as generously as she. Though she suffered great pain, she was a happy, fulfilled woman.

Prayer and Progress • There was another aspect of Catherine's life in which she wanted to be a model for those who came after her. She even wrote a treatise on the subject. The subject, of course, was prayer, and the treatise was *The Dialogue*. In it she describes the journey of the soul toward God, the stages the soul must pass through as she grows from a life dominated by fear toward a life filled with perfect love. Each step along the way has its own kind of prayer — and as the soul makes her journey, her progress depends on her prayer.

This treatise, written out of love for her followers, is as practical today as it was some six hundred years ago.

The Role of Women • Of all the aspects of Catherine's life, the one that compels our attention today is her role as a woman in the Church. Catherine has been raised to a unique position of prominence because she is one of only two women who have been proclaimed Doctors of the Church. What kind of woman of the Church was she?

It would be hard to characterize her as a feminist by today's standards. She never campaigned for female priests, or any other change in the status of women in the hierarchy. Her orthodoxy was impeccable, as Pope Paul VI pointed out in his proclamation. Her absolute obedience to the pope and her willingness to give everything, even her life, for the Church, showed the depth of her loyalty and won the pope's praise. "What did she mean by renewal and reform of the Church?" he asked. "Certainly not the overthrow of its basic structures, rebellion against the pastors, a free rein for personal charisms, arbitrary innovations in worship and discipline, such as some would like in our day."[1]

Catherine did not write or talk about a new role for women — but she lived it, in the Church and in the world. She was a prominent public figure at a time when prominence and publicity belonged almost exclusively to men. She was no respecter of traditional roles: she taught the teachers; she was "manly" among the men, even when they were fearful; she became knowledgeable, and even authoritative, on affairs of Church and State, traditionally male domains.

It is perhaps significant that she made her first bold moves toward freedom after her father died and her brothers were forced to leave Siena when their dye business suffered as a result of political power changing hands.

As has been pointed out, Catherine grew up in a society where women were expected to stay at home and take care of their families' needs. Excursions out in public were considered suspect and damaged a woman's reputation, unless the excursions were for one of a very few, rigidly defined purposes, like attending Mass or taking food to the poor. Women's thoughts, concerns, and knowledge, among other things, likewise were expected to stay at home with domestic matters. There were clear lines of distinction between men's affairs and those of women.

Catherine evidently accepted these standards as the way things were. When she was a young child, she had a fantasy about disguising herself as a male so she could become a Dominican friar; but when she was an adult and Jesus told her that He wanted her to go out into the world as a preacher, she protested, asking how she, an ignorant woman, could do such a thing.

The answer Jesus gave to that question defined the pattern for Catherine's public life. "In my eyes there is neither male nor female, rich nor poor, but all are equal," He said, "for I can do all things with equal ease. I spread abroad the grace of my Spirit where I will. . . . Be brave and obedient when I send you out among people. Wherever you go I will not forsake you, I will be with you, as is my custom, and will guide you in all that you are to do."[2]

As Catherine lived out those instructions, she blazed a new trail for women. She was not looking at the conventions of society and violating them because they were too restrictive. She was not looking at the conventions at all. She was looking at Jesus and listening to Him, and following Him as well as she knew how.

Catherine was not rebellious, but she was revolutionary. She created a new way of living, not just for herself, but for Alessia, and Cecca, and Lisa, and all her other women friends. They all enjoyed freedom they would never have known without Catherine: freedom to travel, freedom to learn, freedom to try new things. The men in the group found new freedom through Catherine, too: freedom to learn from the greatest teacher of their time, freedom to hear the Gospel interpreted from a feminine perspective, freedom to have a woman as a friend.

Perfected by Grace • Catherine created a new role for women in the Church as she created a new role for women in life. Jesus told her, "I spread abroad the grace of my Spirit where I will." As she and her friends opened themselves to receive that grace, they found new roles for themselves, new freedoms, a whole new richness in their lives.

"Humanity perfected by grace," Pope John Paul II called it, and he was awed by the prospect: "the extraordinary richness of humanity, not dimmed in any way, but on the contrary increased and perfected by grace. . . ."[3]

There is no limit to the heights we can reach if, like Catherine, we love God and allow Him to pour His grace into every part of our life and our being. That is the role-model Catherine can be to all of us.

She once said to Stephen Maconi, "If you are what you must be, you will set all of Italy on fire."

If we all, inspired by Catherine, became all that we must be, God could kindle in us a fire so great that together we could renew the face of the earth.

Chapter Notes

Chapter 1

1. *Legend*,* Pt. 1, Ch. 3, No. 35.
2. Ibid., No. 38.
3. Ibid., Ch. 1, No. 23.
4. Ibid., Ch. 4, No. 45.
5. Ibid., No. 49.
6. Ibid., Ch. 5, No. 53.
7. Ibid., No. 54.
8. Ibid., No. 55

Chapter 2

1. *The Dialogue*, p. 63.
2. *Legend*, Pt. 1, Ch. 6, No. 67.
3. Scudder, p. 186.
4. *Legend*, Pt. 1, Ch. 7, No. 72.
5. Jorgensen, pp. 30-32.
6. *Legend*, Pt. 1, Ch. 6, No. 66.
7. Ibid., Ch. 9, No. 84.

---

*NOTE: In the Chapter Notes, *Legend* refers to the official biography of Saint Catherine written by Blessed Raymond of Capua and listed in the Bibliography under his family name — Raymond deVigne.

8. Ibid., Ch. 11, No. 110.
9. Jorgensen, p. 54.
10. *Legend*, Pt. 1, Ch. 12, Nos. 114-115.

Chapter 3

1. *Legend*, Pt. 2, Ch. 1, Nos. 121-122.
2. Drane, p. 58.
3. Ibid., p. 61.
4. Ibid., pp. 62-63.
5. Ibid., p. 62.
6. Ibid., p. 74.
7. *Legend*, Pt. 2, Ch. 4, Nos. 162-163.
8. Ibid., Nos. 147-151.
9. Ibid., Ch. 7, No. 221.

Chapter 4

1. Drane, p. 115.
2. Ibid., pp. 111-112.
3. Ibid., pp. 91-92.

Chapter 5

1. *Legend*, Pt. 2, Ch. 8, Nos. 254-255.
2. Ibid., Nos. 252-253.
3. Ibid., Nos. 246-248.
4. Ibid., Pt. 1, Ch. 9, No. 90.
5. Jorgensen, pp. 258-260.
6. Drane, p. 296.
7. *Legend*, Pt. 2, Ch. 6, Nos. 196-198.
8. Drane, p. 269.

Chapter 6

1. *The Dialogue*, pp. 115-116.
2. Jorgensen, p. 143.
3. Scudder, p. 111.
4. Drane, p. 294.
5. Scudder, pp. 167-171.
6. Jorgensen, p. 207.

Chapter 7

1. Jorgensen, p. 146.
2. Scudder, p. 131.
3. Jorgensen, p. 200.
4. Ibid., pp. 219-220.
5. Drane, pp. 223-225.
6. Ibid., pp. 246-247.
7. Jorgensen, p. 201.
8. Ibid., p. 202.
9. Ibid., p. 200.
10. *Legend*, Pt. 2, Ch. 10, No. 285.

Chapter 8

1. Scudder, pp. 126-128.
2. Drane, p. 303.
3. Ibid., p. 239.
4. Ibid., p. 333.
5. Ibid., p. 334.
6. Ibid., p. 341.

Chapter 9

1. Drane, p. 456.
2. Ibid.

3. Scudder, p. 246.
4. Jorgensen, p. 330.
5. Drane, p. 549.
6. Ibid.
7. Ibid., p. 568.

Chapter 10

1. *Legend*, Pt. 3, Ch. 5, No. 378.

Chapter 11

1. *Legend*, Pt. 1, Ch. 6, No. 198.
2. Scudder, p. 231.
3. Ibid., pp. 160-161.

Chapter 12

1. *L'Osservatore Romano*, October 15, 1970. (All quotations from Pope Paul VI come from this issue of *L'Osservatore*.)
2. Jorgensen, p. 66.
3. *L'Osservatore Romano*, October 15, 1970.
4. Ibid.
5. Ibid.
6. Ibid.
7. Ibid.
8. Ibid.
9. Ibid.
10. Ibid.
11. Ibid., April 28, 1980.
12. Ibid.
13. Ibid.
14. Ibid.

15. Ibid.
16. Ibid., June 23, 1980.
17. Ibid., July 14, 1980.
18. Ibid., September 22, 1980.
19. Ibid.

Chapter 13

1. Scudder, p. 26.
2. *The Dialogue*, p. 29.
3. Ibid., p. 31.
4. Ibid., p. 26.
5. Scudder, p. 144.
6. *The Dialogue*, p. 91.
7. Ibid., pp. 28-29.
8. Ibid., pp. 42-43.
9. Ibid., p. 28.
10. Ibid., pp. 157-158.
11. Ibid., p. 126.
12. Ibid., p. 148.
13. *Legend*, Pt. 2, Ch. 6, No. 185.
14. *The Dialogue*, p. 221.
15. Ibid., p. 138.
16. *Legend*, Pt. 2, Ch. 6, No. 187.

Chapter 14

1. *L'Osservatore Romano*, October 15, 1970.
2. *Legend*, Pt. 2, Ch. 1, Nos. 121-122.
3. *L'Osservatore Romano*, June 23, 1980.

Bibliography

Bell, Rudolph M. *Holy Anorexia*. Chicago: The University of Chicago Press, 1985.

Benincasa, Catherine. *The Prayers of Catherine of Siena*. Edited by Suzanne Noffke, O.P. New York: Paulist Press, 1983.

_____. *The Dialogue*. Translation and introduction by Suzanne Noffke, O.P. New York: Paulist Press, 1980.

Bruch, Hilde, M.D. *The Golden Cage: The Enigma of Anorexia Nervosa*. Cambridge, Mass.: Harvard University Press, 1978.

Drane, Augusta Theodosia. *The History of St. Catherine of Siena*. London: Burns and Oates, 1880.

Fatula, Mary Ann, O.P. "Catherine of Siena on the Communion of Friendship," in *Review for Religious* (March, 1984).

Follmar, Mary Ann, O.P. *Catherine of Siena and Julian of Norwich: A Message of Hope for the Church*. Rome: Curia Generalizia O.P., 1981.

Gillet, Martin S., O.P. *The Mission of St. Catherine*. Translated by Sister M. Thomas López, O.P. St. Louis, Mo.: B. Herder Book Co., 1955.

Jacobus de Voragine. *The Golden Legend*. Translated and adapted from the Latin by Granger Ryan and Helmut Ripperger. New York: Longmans, Green and Co., 1941.

Jorgensen, Johannes. *Saint Catherine of Siena*. Translated from the Danish by Ingeborg Lund. New York: Longmans, Green and Co., 1938.

Knowles, David. *Christian Monasticism*. New York: McGraw-Hill Book Co., 1969.

Larner, John. *Italy in the Age of Dante and Petrarch: 1216-1380*. A Longman History of Italy Series, Vol. 2. New York: Longman, 1980.

The Lives of the Desert Fathers. Translated by Norman Russell. London and Oxford: Mowbray; Kalamazoo, Mich.: Cistercian Publications, 1980.

Noffke, Suzanne, O.P. "Catherine of Siena: Mission and Ministry in the Church," in *Review for Religious* (March, 1980).

L'Osservatore Romano, October 15, 1970; April 28, 1980; June 23, 1980; July 14, 1980; September 22, 1980.

Saint Dominic Biographical Documents. Edited with an Introduction by Francis C. Lehner, O.P. Washington, D.C.: The Thomist Press, 1964.

Scudder, Vida. *Saint Catherine of Siena as Seen in Her Letters*. New York: E.P. Dutton and Co., 1926.

Taurisano, Innocenzio. *The Little Flowers of Saint Catherine of Siena*. Translated from the Italian by Charlotte Dease. St. Paul, Minn.: The E.M. Lohmann Co., n.d.

Trollope, T. Adolphus. *A Decade of Italian Women*. Vol. 1. London: Chapman and Hall, 1859.

deVigne, Raymond. *The Life of Catherine of Siena*. Translated, introduced, and annotated by Conleth Kearns, O.P. Wilmington, Del.: Michael Glazier, Inc., 1980.

_____. *The Life of St. Catherine of Siena*. Translated by George Lamb. New York: Kenedy, 1960.